Ronald W. West

AROUND
THE
SOUND

AROUND THE SOUND

A History of Howe Sound– Whistler

Doreen Armitage

HARBOUR PUBLISHING

Harbour Publishing
P.O. Box 219
Madeira Park, BC
V0N 2H0
Canada

THE CANADA COUNCIL | LE CONSEIL DES ARTS
FOR THE ARTS | DU CANADA
SINCE 1957 | DEPUIS 1957

Published with the assistance of the Canada Council and the Province
of British Columbia through the British Columbia Arts Council

Cover, maps, page design and composition by
Martin Nichols, Lionheart Graphics
Cover photo by Tim Turner
Printed and bound in Canada

Key to photograph sources: AM: Amy Martin Collection; BB: Brunswick
Beach Community Collection; BCARS: BC Archives & Records Service;
BCF: BC Ferries; BCH: BC Hydro; BIH: Bowen Island Historians;
BIH/DH: Dale Harding Collection, Bowen Island Historians; CVA: City of
Vancouver Archives; DA: Doreen Armitage photograph; EPM:
Elphinstone Pioneer Museum Collection; JA: Justine Armstrong
Collection; KC: Keats Camps Collection; MK: Marie Kendall Collection;
Pay: Pay Family Collection; PM: Phyllis Malm Collection; SPL:
Squamish Public Library; UBC: University of British Columbia Library,
Special Collections; UBC/MB: University of BC Library, Special
Collections, MacMillan Bloedel Collection; UBC/Spils: University of BC
Library, Special Collections, Spilsbury Papers; VAQ: Vancouver
Aquarium Collection; VPL: Vancouver Public Library; WMA: Whistler
Museum and Archives Collection.

Canadian Cataloguing in Publication Data

Armitage, Doreen, 1931–
    Around the Sound

    Includes bibliographical references and index.
    ISBN 1-55017-235-2

    1. Howe Sound Region (B.C.)—History. 2. Whistler (B.C.)—
History. I. Title.
FC3845.H69A77 1997   971.1.'31   C97-910758-X
F1089.H69A77 1997

to Bill

ACKNOWLEDGEMENTS

I extend my deep appreciation to the following people who have contributed to the contents of this book:

Lola and Jim Westell of Elphinstone Pioneer Museum at Gibsons who were always there when I needed information; Dorothy Lawson and the volunteers at the Bowen Island Archives; Sherry Elchuk, BC Museum of Mining at Britannia Beach; Bettina Fallon, Whistler Museum and Archives; Rupert Harrison, Honorary Archivist, West Vancouver; and the staffs at the University of British Columbia Library, Special Collections, the City of Vancouver Archives and the Vancouver Public Library.

For the wonderful stories they shared with me: Justine Armstrong, Bowyer Island; George and Barbara Brooks, scuba diving; Gerry Chaster, Cheakamus Power Project and highway surveying; Jim Elliott, Britannia and Squamish; Bill Flett, Cheakamus Power Project; Donald Graham, Point Atkinson; Marie Kendall, Anvil Island; Phyllis Malm, Britannia and Woodfibre; Amy Martin and Doreen Bowman, Green Lake, Whistler; Hanna Swanson, Britannia; Rose Tatlow, Squamish; Joan Tennant, Bowen Island; and Nicol Warn, Gambier Island.

For their expert advice: Ross Carter, Bowen Island; John Clague, Geological Survey of Canada; Jeff Marliave, Vancouver Aquarium; Mike Nassichuk, Environment Canada; and Bruce Nidle, Fisheries and Oceans Canada.

For their willingness to share their time and knowledge: Leiani Anthony, Gambier Island; Rob Bentall, Keats Island; Pat Crawford, Information Services, BC Hydro; Ron Copp, Brunswick Beach; Vince Ivancic, Western Pulp Inc., Woodfibre; Ian MacDonald, West Vancouver; and Kirk Potter, Keats Camps.

For their kindness in providing photographs: Bill Dale, Woodfibre, and Betty Pay, Eastbourne, Keats Island.

And to my good friend Elspeth Bradbury, whose encouragement started me off and kept me going.

Doreen Armitage

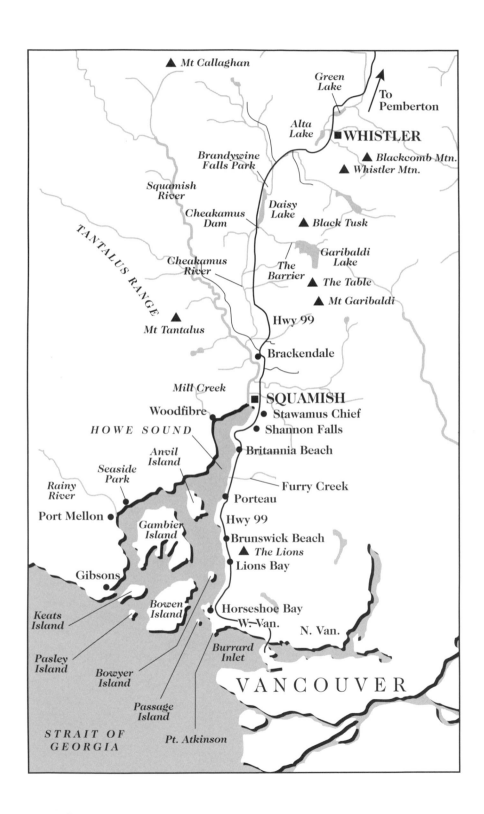

CONTENTS

INTRODUCTION

Where Howe Sound's southern boundary meets the Strait of Georgia, the waves, white-capped from the Squamish winds, wash Point Atkinson's rocky buttresses, break on Bowen Island's southern shore, and hiss through the stony shingle at Gower Point near Gibsons. The magnificent natural environment in the area known as Sea to Sky Country stretches northeast from there to Whistler and beyond. Nestled between Howe Sound's two shorelines, which reach out like welcoming arms, are tree-clad islands attracting those looking for secluded settings close to Vancouver. The highway from West Vancouver follows the base of the Coast Mountains and winds through some of the most spectacular scenery in the world: snow-capped extinct volcanoes, glaciers, lush forests, and lakes and rivers ranging in colour from deep blue to a milky green, silty from the snow runoff.

This is a land of superlatives—the best skiing in North America, the best windsurfing in Canada, the first underwater marine park in Canada (from which no sea life may be removed), the largest eagle population in North America and the second largest granite monolith in the world.

The combination of mountains and water has produced an environment that could also be named "Super Sports Country." From scuba diving in Howe Sound's depths to heli-skiing in the mountains, sports enthusiasts can take their choice of enjoyment in the outdoors—hiking, mountaineering, ice and rock climbing, skiing, mountain biking, sailing and kayaking.

The mountainous terrain is a major attraction, but is far from benign. It has precipitated death and destruction through rockfalls, floods and debris torrents from the rushing mountain creeks. The highway, cut

An early photo (probably in the 1940s) looking up Howe Sound. Passage Island, named by Captain George Vancouver in 1792, is shown in the centre. The island marks the southeastern entrance to Howe Sound through Queen Charlotte Channel. Bowen Island can be seen at left and Whytecliff Park at middle right. *(VPL 16447)*

through bedrock and winding high above Howe Sound and through the narrow Cheakamus Canyon, has been the scene of hundreds of traffic injuries and deaths.

The story of Howe Sound, its islands, shoreline and neighbouring lands and mountains, is a story of people and the events that shaped their lives. Much of it is told in their own words—the words of the Squamish people, settlers, loggers, prospectors and those in search of the pleasures of life in the great outdoors.

This is also a story of giving and taking and giving back. The early glaciation and volcanic eruptions uncovered rich ore beds. The land gave to the people and they mined copper, silver and gold. The moderate climate produced giant cedars, hemlocks and firs, and the people logged the forests and built homes and boats. The lush river valleys and fertile fields gave to the people, and they harvested fruits and vegetables. The water of lakes, rivers and ocean gave sea life and attracted waterbirds and mammals, and the people flourished on nature's abundance. There was so much for the taking.

For many years the people have been in the process of giving back through reforestation, conservation and environmental protection. They care enough to make a difference. The land is, again, receiving.

CHAPTER 1

FROM THE SEA TO THE SKY

In the beginning there was water everywhere and no land at all. When this state of things had lasted for a long while, the Great Spirit determined to make land appear. Soon the tops of the mountains showed above the water and they grew and grew till their heads reached the clouds. Then he made the lakes and rivers, and after that the trees and animals.

—Mulks, 100-year-old elder of the Squamish Nation, dictated in archaic Coast Salish, 1896 (In *The Salish People*, vol. II, by Charles Hill-Tout)

I f you had been living in the land we now call British Columbia about 30,000 years ago, you probably wouldn't have noticed the gradual weather change or been able to predict the awesome transformation that was about to take place. Plants similar to those in today's temperate forests carpeted the hills and river valleys. Animals roamed the forests, but many of them, like the mammoths, are extinct today.

Slowly but relentlessly the climate grew colder. Heavier and more frequent snowfalls built up expanding snowbanks. Small glaciers formed in hollows on the mountainsides. High up on the mountain peaks of the Tantalus and Coast ranges, existing glaciers spread downward, freezing the green hillsides. A new ice age was changing the face of the landscape, and glaciers from several mountain ranges would eventually join together to cover most of British Columbia, Yukon and Alaska, western Alberta and the northwestern United States under a massive ice sheet.

Over the next 15,000 years, you could have watched great lobes of ice spill into the valleys and follow the routes of ancient river beds. A major glacier, about 2000 metres (6500 feet) thick, deepened and widened the

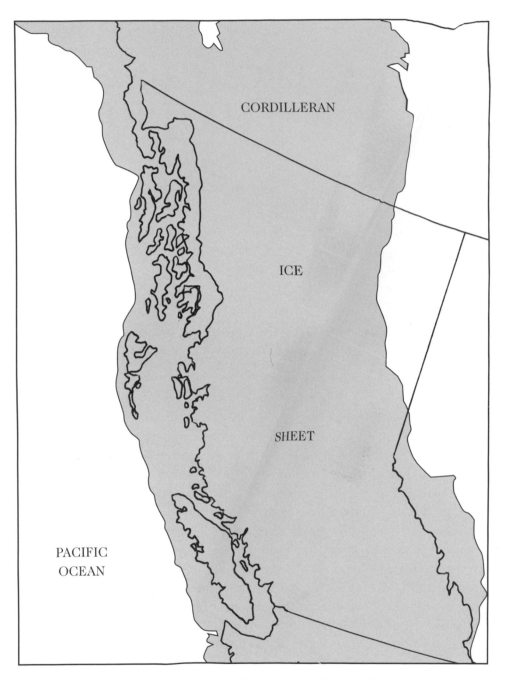

CORDILLERAN

ICE

SHEET

PACIFIC
OCEAN

About 30,000 years ago, the weather in what is now the British Columbia area began to grow colder. Frequent and heavy snowfalls caused glaciers to spread from the mountains into the valleys, finally covering most of present-day BC in a layer of ice so thick that most of the mountains were covered. *(Courtesy John J. Clague)* valleys around the Squamish and Cheakamus Rivers, then pushed through the river valley that is now Howe Sound. Streams of meltwater from the glacier carried sand and gravel to the fan-shaped plains that had built up in the Strait of Georgia, formerly an inland sea.[1] Only the highest peaks, like the Lions and Whistler Mountain, appeared as islands above the massive ice sheet. Eventually, about 15,000 years ago, the area sagged under the weight of millions of tonnes of ice.[2]

If you had been an observer, you would not have noticed the next gradual climate change as the glaciers began to melt and recede. The rasping tongue of the Howe Sound and Squamish Valley glacier pulled back from the abraded remains of low mountains—now islands named Bowen and Bowyer, Keats, Anvil and Gambier—leaving its signature on scarred cliffs like the Stawamus Chief in Squamish and depositing rock and gravel in its wake.

When the ice had retreated as far north as what is now Porteau Cove, a cooler period slowed the melt for some time. Rock debris was released from the melting ice and built up a ridge or "sill" that formed a curve across Howe Sound. (Later, the ridge attracted rich marine life to the shallower water, which, in turn, attracts adventurous divers today who explore the underwater bounty.)

You would have heard the frigid landscape resounding with the boom of house-size chunks of ice splitting from the glacier and dropping into the encroaching sea. The splash of meltwater, eroding the ice's exposed surface, provided a continuous chorus. But the most spectacular display was yet to come.

The peak of a broad volcanic cone that reached above the massive ice field erupted into flame, as though in retaliation for the glacier's long suppression. The relentless force of fire fought the ice to herald Mount Garibaldi's birth. Avalanches of boiling lava, spitting sparks and flame from the intense heat, roared across the glacier, while dense clouds of steam and hot ash blotted out the sky. Rocks and ash billowed down the sides of the growing mountain dome, intermingling with the solid remains of cooled lava. Finally a cone made up of rocks and ash, enclosing an area of 6 cubic kilometres (1.5 cubic miles), stood triumphant above the smoke and flames.

Where fire and ice met, the lava and ash seemed victorious, blanketing large sections of the glacier, but the passive glacial melt and retreat claimed the final victory. As the supporting ice diminished, removing the foundation for the volcanic debris, tremendous rock slides thundered into the valley, carrying with them almost half of the existing cone. Today, about 26 square kilometres (10 square miles) of the Squamish Valley floor rest on a 91-metre-thick (300 foot) base of rocks and rubble that once formed Mount Garibaldi's western slope. The mountain is much less than its original height, at 2678 metres (8787 feet). It is the only known, major, Pleistocene age volcano in North America that actually built itself upon a glacier.[3]

During the same period, another battle between fire and ice was taking place just north of Mount Garibaldi. It molded an unusual, flat-topped lava formation called The Table, which rises vertically several hundred metres above the valley floor. The volcano repeatedly spewed flaming lava into a hole melted in the glacier. Over time this built up a series of round horizontal sheets enclosed by ice walls, with lava flows solidifying around the sides of the sheets, like layers of pancakes dripping with syrup.

Throughout the Garibaldi Volcanic Belt from Squamish to Meager Mountain north of Pemberton, lava flows and rock debris created mountains, lakes and unusual landforms—Black Tusk, Cinder Cone, Mount Price and Mount Cayley to name a few—that now attract thousands of hikers and climbers annually. Lobes of molten lava blocked a valley and formed a basin that now holds Garibaldi Lake. Other rivers of lava solidified against the ice near Rubble Creek Valley. The lava flows cooled rapidly as they met the cold barrier, forming steep cliff faces.[4] As the lava's heat melted the ice, more lava, like liquid wax, filled the vertical spaces. The result was a spectacular 500-metre (1640-foot) cliff that rises from the valley floor and barricades the water of Garibaldi Lake. This barricade partially collapsed in the 1850s, causing a dramatic change in the landscape just before the first white men explored the Squamish and Cheakamus Valleys.

Leaving some small glaciers high in the mountains, the Squamish Valley lobe of the ice sheet gradually disappeared. The weight of the ice had depressed the newly uncovered land by several hundred metres. As the ice melted and the water returned to the sea, you would have witnessed another spectacular display as icy saltwater poured inland over the depressed land, raising the sea about 200 metres (660 feet) higher than today's level.

About 10,000 years ago, when the land had finally regained its original

Black Tusk, a dramatic peak formed when Mount Garibaldi erupted while the area was still covered by a glacier. Mount Garibaldi and another lava formation, The Table, can be seen in the background. *(UBC/Spils)*

The Table, in Garibaldi Park, built up by successive layers of lava. Each layer was cooled by the surrounding glacier before being covered by a new layer. *(UBC/Spils)*

Bricklike formations of columnar basalt, made of lava exuded by the Garibaldi volcano. This area is very popular with geologists. *(UBC/Spils)*

height, an equilibrium was established and the water receded. Remains of sea life blanketed the ground and may still be found in fossils south of Squamish.

The tumult died. Peace spread over the mountains and islands, waterfalls and rivers. Seedlings hesitantly sent feelers out around the barren rocks. Lichens and mosses carpeted the ground. You would have seen forests of alder, willow, lodgepole pine and buffalo berry greening the hillsides. Much later, Douglas fir, western red cedar and other conifers reached for the skies—a rain forest was in the making. When the earliest white settlers visited Sea to Sky Country in the 1800s, they encountered the same types of soaring trees and lush mosses, ferns and bushes as had existed thousands of years before.[5]

The First People

While the slow process of glacial melt was uncovering the land, the first pioneers entered British Columbia by crossing the Bering Land Bridge. Travelling slowly south along an ice-free route from the Yukon, hunting and gathering along the way, they established territories throughout North America. Archaeologists studying shell middens in and around Vancouver have dated native occupation there from as long as 9000 years ago.[6] The culture of these people evolved into what we know today as the Coast Salish and Squamish nations.

The Coast Salish language, used by the Squamish people, is similar to that of First Nations people in Washington state, just south of the border between Canada and the United States. The Washington natives believed that the Squamish originated from the bands in that state. They

A glacier near The Table, c. 1950. Most of the massive ice cover in the Garibaldi area melted some 10,000 years ago, but several glaciers still remain in the mountains. During the fifty years prior to this photo, the glacier had receded all the way from the treeline (centre). *(UBC/Spils)*

tell a story about some of their people who, on a fishing trip along the coast, were blown to Point Grey in a storm and settled there.

In reality, some bands of adventurous hunters left their settlements on the upper Fraser and Thompson Rivers and, following valleys and streams, gradually worked their way southwards. Their stories of limitless game and fish spread back to other nomadic groups who were constantly moving in search of food. Some of them discovered the lush Squamish Valley and recognized it as the ideal location for their homes. Fish abounded in the lakes, rivers and ocean, game was plentiful, and the rich land provided roots and berries for food and cedar for their winter homes.

The Squamish territory eventually extended throughout Howe Sound and Burrard Inlet, from Gibsons at the southwestern end of the sound north to the Shovel Nose Indian Reserve on the Squamish River. To the east it reached Port Moody and the Indian River. Some believe Point Grey was the southern boundary; others feel that it stretched to Musqueam.

Over the years, the Squamish people named many villages and

geographical features around Vancouver, Howe Sound and the upper Squamish Valley, each descriptive of its locale. A legend about twin girls gave the name Chee-Chee, meaning twins, to the two peaks (now called the Lions) that can be seen from Vancouver. The bay at Gibsons was called Scjunk, meaning "a fellow is standing up and watching out (leaning against a big rock)," because a big rock lies on the shore at the middle of the bay. Port Graves on Gambier Island was known as Charl-Kunch, "(long) deep bay," and Passage Island, near Point Atkinson, was named Smismus-Sulch, "the waves go over it all the time."

A 1975 British Columbia Archaeological Survey uncovered evidence of several native camps or villages on islands in the Sound: on Gambier Island there were 19 sites; 5 sites on Keats Island; Bowen Island, 10 sites; Pasley Island, 7; Shelter and Hermit Islands, 1 each. Within the town of Gibsons, 10 sites produced artifacts. Shell middens, granite hammers, a basalt point adze and many chipped points showed where native people had lived and hunted. In 1981, the Worrall burial site at Gower Point near Gibsons disclosed scattered remains of a native male, aged 20 to 30 years, likely prehistoric and probably part of a burial site.

Around the year 1800, at least 16 villages existed on the Squamish River within 40 kilometres (25 miles) of its mouth, but their inhabitants mainly used summer sites on Burrard Inlet or Howe Sound.[7]

Natives from the Chekwelp reserve between Granthams Landing and Gibson's Landing c. 1913. *(EPM)*

Within these boundaries the Squamish people pursued their daily activities, camping during the summer under light shelters made of woven mats or in huts made of slabs of cedar bark supported by poles. In winter they lived in roomy lodges consisting of a permanent post-and-beam framework enclosed by a removable cover of roof and wall cedar planks. The homes were parallel to the shore, near the water where the residents could beach their canoes. Each family in the local group occupied one section of the winter house. The wife, husband, unmarried children, older relatives and slaves shared their own fire, cooking and eating their personal food supplies separate from the others in the dwelling. The lodges provided cozy settings for songs, stories and spirit dances during the long, cold, wet nights. The same village sites endured for hundreds of years.

The Squamish men practised polygamy, and a chief often had four or five wives. The women prepared most of the meals, collected and dried berries for use in flat cakes, and dug edible roots using sharp sticks. After preparing the morning meal, the women swept out their dwellings with boughs, then, constantly busy, would weave mats, baskets and blankets while their children played noisily throughout the camp.

When the time came for a woman to deliver her baby, she would go out to a quiet spot in the woods where friends helped her to build a small tent of woven cedar mats, then assisted in the delivery. Babies' heads were permanently flattened by the pressure of cedar-bark pads in their cradles. This practice was important because a flattened head signified nonslave status.

During the winter the men hunted in the surrounding forests. In summer the families canoed to camps on English Bay and Burrard Inlet, where they fished and gathered berries. These were favourite locations for their traditional method of hunting ducks. In the evening the hunters prepared narrow, specially built, duck-hunting canoes by placing a cedar slab covered with mud across the gunwales of each one, then built a fire on top of the mud. At dusk they paddled silently, waiting. When the flames encouraged the ducks to investigate more closely, the hunter in the bow steadied his spear, attached to the end of a long pole. A sharp, expert jab and one more duck was ready for the coals.

The Squamish people treated salmon with great reverence. At the yearly First Salmon Ceremony, the children carried in the specially prepared fish. After everyone had eaten with solemn care, they followed a time-honoured ritual as they returned the bones to the water. They believed that the salmon lived in their own world as people, but appeared each year as fish to provide their flesh to humans. The Squamish smoked this staple food over alder or hemlock fires and were able to store it dried for up to two years, often having about a hundred salmon stored safely for the winter. It remained "hard as a bone." They soaked it in water before preparing it for eating.

The men also hunted and fished near their villages on the Squamish and Cheakamus Rivers. The word "Cheakamus" means "basket catch fish" (or "salmon weir place") in the Salish language. During spawning season on the Squamish and Fraser Rivers, giant sturgeon weighing as much as 270 kilograms (600 pounds) succumbed to the fishermen's long-handled harpoons, which were connected to floats and lanyards.[8]

One large settlement at Horseshoe Bay was a popular fishing locale for the Squamish, who were attracted by the large number of smelts. In fact, the native name for Horseshoe Bay is Cha-Hai, which means "that peculiar sizzling noise, similar to that made when frying bacon in a pan, but which is made by myriads of small fish—smelts do it—moving in the water."

Sea otters did not come into Howe Sound, but the abundance of seals provided a good source of meat. As they slept just under the rolling surface of the water or on the rocks east of Bowen Island, the native hunters would approach quietly in their canoes and spear them. The subsequent celebration of the fresh catch involved a traditional cooking method. While their families waited in anticipation, the hunters would lay a seal across two logs, between which a small fire burned. As the hair scorched off, they turned the body over by holding the head and tail. This allowed for slow cooking. After the middle was done, they cooked the head, then the tail, the same way. A mouthwatering feast ensued.

Although the ocean and rivers provided their major sustenance, hunters also roamed the forests in search of animals for hides and meat. Large herds of elk in the forest bordering Point Grey and False Creek, and mountain goats attracted the hunters. Deer also were abundant, and the men tracked them with their dogs. Venison was roasted on an indoor fire. The cook pierced the meat with a sharp stick, then placed the stick upright in the earth, close to the coals. To boil meat they would heat rocks in the fire, place them in a cedar trough full of water, then add the meat. The women served the meat and vegetables on a large wooden platter about one metre (three feet) long. The family would sit around the serving platter on mats and low wooden blocks. They used stone knives and mountain-goat-horn spoons to eat.

A story, passed down through generations, told of a grizzly bear as tall as two men, killed by one of the hunters near the Squamish villages. The hunter cut the grizzly in half and covered the door of his cedar house with the hide. As this happened before the coming of the white man, the hunter must have used a spear or arrows, which made the accomplishment even more outstanding.

The natives' lives were not always peaceful and productive. The men sometimes fought with their northern neighbours, the St'at'imc (Lillooets), and defended their villages from bands of Tsilhqot'in (Chilcotin) people and ferocious Lekwiltok (Ukeltaws) who would take slaves and massacre the rest of the village.

Farther inland, some of the St'at'imc people lived in the vicinity of Whistler, camping on the shores of Green Lake and the upper Squamish and Lillooet Rivers, but their main villages extended to the north and east of Pemberton. They hunted along the upper reaches of the Squamish, the Mamquam, and other rivers flowing into Howe Sound. Their relationship with the Squamish must have been reasonably friendly, since intermarriages were common enough that numerous St'at'imc families had relatives among the Squamish tribe. Many St'at'imc wives settled with their Squamish husbands, and several families spoke the St'at'imcets language between themselves.[9]

So time passed until the white man came, bringing gifts of clothing, food and hunting tools, and the horrors of smallpox and tuberculosis.

Captain George Vancouver arrived in 1792. Native tradition prophesied a calamity every seven years (measured by the changing phases of the moon and the passing seasons), and Vancouver's arrival coincided with a seventh year. The Squamish passed on to their children and children's children the story of Vancouver's special welcome. As his boats passed through the First Narrows, the natives paddled out to greet him in their canoes and threw clouds of white feathers into the air. The feathers settled like snowflakes on the water. This ceremonious welcome, plus the gifts of fish to the white men, convinced Captain Vancouver that the natives were friendly, but he could not have guessed their underlying purpose. As this was a seventh year, the Squamish were beseeching the visitors to have pity on them and their families.

CHAPTER 2

THE SEEKERS

The gap we had entered in the snowy barrier seemed of little importance, as through the vallies, caused by the irregularity of the mountain's tops, other mountains more distant, and apparently more elevated, were seen rearing their lofty heads in various directions.

—Captain George Vancouver, surveying in
Howe Sound, Friday, June 15, 1792

Who was the first overseas traveller to marvel at the awesome, rugged beauty of Sea to Sky Country? We naturally think of Captain Vancouver as the earliest explorer to survey Howe Sound and the Lower Mainland coast in 1792. However, fascinating stories of mysterious, long-haired, white dogs, troves of ancient Chinese coins and oriental carvings found on the coast point to much more ancient visitors.

In 1920, William Wyton made a surprising discovery at Hopkins Landing on Howe Sound's western shore. He was probably clearing land for his ranch, on his knees, prying at the roots of a giant fir stump, when he noticed a tiny, irregularly shaped object. Rubbing away the accumulation of earth, he puzzled over what appeared to be a detailed carving. At home, his careful cleaning revealed a 6.3-centimetre-high (2½-inch), pale yellowish-green jade monkey—the "speak no evil" of a set of "hear no evil, see no evil, speak no evil" so popular in China. It became a prized family possession. Archaeological staff at the University of British Columbia later identified China as its place of origin and estimated its age at 1500 years. We will never know how it found its way to Howe Sound. Did coastal natives obtain it in trade, or did the Chinese carry it to its final resting place? However it travelled, it is now a treasured exhibit at the Elphinstone Pioneer Museum in Gibsons.

Coincidentally, 1500 years ago, in AD 499, about the same time that an Asian sculptor created the monkey, a Chinese Buddhist monk named

Hoei-shin entered the details of his journey to Fusang, a country far to the east of China, into the annals of the Chinese Empire. Historian John K. Lord, writing in the 1880s, claimed that words of Japanese origin were used in the Chinook jargon spoken on the coast, and west coast history contains many reliable reports of shipwrecks of Japanese and Chinese junks.[1]

Perhaps the most unusual proof of early Asian visitors comes from European explorers' stories of white, woolly dogs owned by coastal tribes who kept the dogs on isolated islands so they were unable to escape. Lord also wrote about these animals, describing them as very different from the tamed coyotes or wolves found living with interior bands. Similar dogs were common

This 2 1/2-inch tall jade, "Speak No Evil" carving was dug up from under a fir stump in Hopkins Landing in 1920. Its age was estimated at 1500 years. *(EPM)*

in Japan, so the ones living in west coast villages could have come to the coast with Japanese sailors. If so, the sailors had evidently taught the natives the art of weaving the hair, later a popular trade item, into clothing and blankets.

Much later, from the sixteenth to the nineteenth centuries, explorers searched for the Strait of Anian, the elusive Northwest Passage. Ships from Spain, England and Russia travelled the coast, but the range of islands to the west of the mainland effectively concealed the existence of what we now know as the Strait of Georgia and its neighbouring waters. Finally, in 1791, Spanish explorers visited the strait and explored at least some of adjoining Howe Sound, naming several geographical features. The next year their compatriots prepared the first chart of the area, inscribing the names assigned the previous year. Among others, the Strait of Georgia was El Gran Canal de Nuestra Senora del Rosario de Marinera (the Great Channel of Our Lady of the Rosary of the Seafarers), Bowen Island and nearby islands, the first land in Howe Sound to receive

Painting showing Captain George Vancouver's small boats entering Burrard Inlet in 1792, while charting the area. *(UBC BC1060)*

a European name, were the Islas de Apodaca (Islands of Apodaca), and Howe Sound itself was called Boca del Carmelo, meaning "mouth or entrance to Carmel," after the biblical Mount Carmel.[2] The names were to have a short life. The next year the British would give some of the same geographical features English names.

Captain George Vancouver, born to a Dutch family in England, was in charge of a British voyage to carry out a four-and-a-half-year hydrographic survey, one of the longest ever launched. He and his crew entered the "Gran Canal" in June 1792 and, not aware that it had already been named, christened it the Gulph of Georgia in honour of King George III. Sailing slightly to the south, he left his ships, *Discovery* and *Chatham*, at station in Birch Bay. Vancouver and his men set out with a week's provisions in two open boats, the *Discovery*'s yawl and launch, to row and sail around the shores of the main inlets of the Gulph, as the small boats could enter shallow channels not accessible to the larger ships. After surveying Burrard's Canal (later changed to Burrard's Channel) as far as what we now call Indian Arm, and trading with the local Squamish natives, Vancouver and his crews retraced their route to the rocky point at the southeastern boundary of Howe Sound and named it Point Atkinson, after a "particular friend," and also called the "low rocky island, producing some trees," to the west, "Passage Island." Still travelling in the open boats, they entered the sound on Thursday, June 14. The

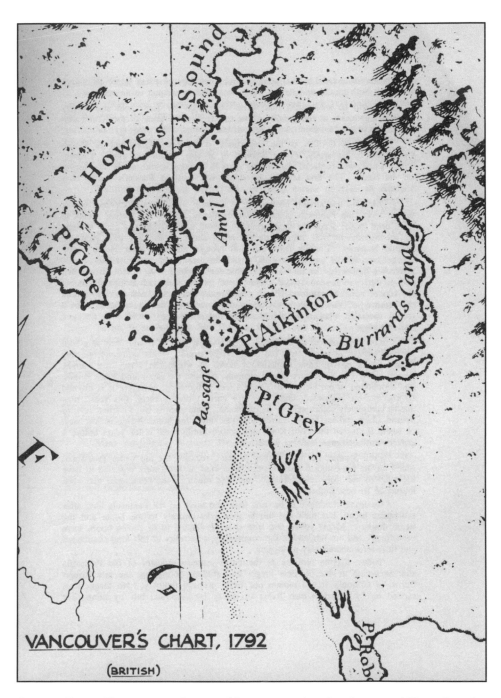

Captain George Vancouver and some of his crew explored and surveyed Howe Sound on June 14 and 15, 1792 in two small ship's boats. He charted and named the sound and some of the islands.

men must have been less than impressed with their surroundings. As Captain Vancouver expressed his perceptions:

Quitting Point Atkinson, and proceeding up the sound . . . we made a rapid progress, by the assistance of a fresh southerly gale, attended with dark gloomy weather, that greatly added to the dreary prospect of the surrounding country. The low fertile shores we had been accustomed to see, though lately with some interruption, here no longer existed; their place was now occupied by the base of the stupendous snowy barrier, thinly wooded, and rising from the sea abruptly to the clouds; from whose frigid summit, the dissolving snow in foaming torrents rushed down the sides and chasms of its rugged surface, exhibiting altogether a sublime, though gloomy spectacle, which animated nature seemed to have deserted. Not a bird, nor living creature was to be seen, and the roaring of the falling cataracts in every direction precluded their being heard, had any been in our neighbourhood.[3]

The expedition's botanist and surgeon, Archibald Menzies, did not accompany the ship's boats into Howe Sound, so we know very little about the flora and fauna at that time. Menzies did include a few details in his journal, obviously from verbal communication with the crews on their return: "some islands all covered with Pines" (although the trees were probably an assortment of cedar, fir and hemlock) and "near the entrance [to Howe Sound] they passed some Rocky Islands on which they shot a few Sea Pies [oyster-catchers]."[4]

Vancouver and his crew were now just over a year into their journey. After months of cramped quarters on board, a rather monotonous diet and limited social interactions, this "dreary prospect" must have been deeply depressing, seeming hardly worth the effort spent on the surveying. Nevertheless, Anvil Island received its name that day, "from the shape of the mountain that composes it." They travelled a little farther north and set up camp.

"In this dreary and comfortless region," Captain Vancouver reported, "it was no inconsiderable piece of good fortune to find a little cove in which we could take shelter, and a small spot of level land on which we could erect our tent; as we had scarcely finished our examination when the wind became excessively boisterous from the southward, attended with heavy squalls and torrents of rain, which continuing until noon the following day, Friday the fifteenth, occasioned a very unpleasant detention."

Vancouver's lieutenant, Peter Puget, was in charge of one of the boats, and in his diary he noted: "We found the termination of the inlet, ending in two shallow bays, with an immense quantity of drift wood on

"High snowy mountains, unfathomable Inlets, with steep Rocky Shores was the only prospect before us," wrote Lt. Peter Puget in his diary on June 14, 1792 when describing Howe Sound. (*Public Records Office, London, England*)

both. We returned three miles down again and pitched the tents early as it had already begun to rain and was likewise blowing hard from the southward. Here we both dried and slept. We could not avoid remarking what a different aspect the country now wore, when compared to the pleasant green plains to the southward. High snowy mountains, unfathomable inlets, with steep rocky shores was the only prospect before us. The change in so small a distance is truly wonderful, even at the termination of these inlets high snowy mountains rise immediately at their back forming a pleasant though romantic appearance."[5] This would have been at the mouth of the Squamish River.

The following morning, again stormy, the men's spirits lifted a little with the visit of about forty natives whose physical appearance, Vancouver decided, was identical to the natives with whom he had traded off the shores of Burrard's Channel. Indeed, they were all Squamish of the Coast Salish tribe. A busy period of trading ensued, with the natives exchanging fish, their garments, spears, bows and arrows, and roughly made copper ornaments for European articles, iron being preferred. So much did they enjoy the experience that they bartered amongst themselves for goods received from the Europeans and traded some back to the sailors when activity slowed down.

Native elders passed down a story to their children about an early visit of white men at Squamish. It could describe the above meeting or another with an earlier or later explorer. In either case, it provides an amusing insight into early contacts with natives. August Jack Khahtsahlano recounted it in his conversations with J.S. Matthews.

I was born at Snauq, the old Indian village under the Burrard bridge. When I little boy I listen old people talk. Old people say Indians see first whitemans up near Squamish. When they see first ship they think it an island with three dead trees, might be schooner, might be sloop; two masts and bowsprit, sails tied up. Indian braves in about twenty canoes come down Squamish river, go see. Get nearer, see men on island, men have black clothes with high hat coming to point at top. Think most likely black uniform and great coat turned up collar like priests cowl. Whitemans give Indians ship's biscuit; Indian not know what biscuit for. Before whitemans come, Indians have little balls, not very big; roll them along ground, shoot at them with bow and arrow for practice, teach young Indian so as not to miss deer. Just the same you use clay pigeon. Indian not know ship's biscuit good to eat, so roll them along ground like little practice balls, shoot at them, break them up. [Sign as of bowling a cricket ball "underhand."]

Then whitemans on schooner give molasses same time biscuit. Indian not know what it for, so Indian rub on leg [thighs and calves] for medicine. You know Indian sit on legs for long time in canoe; legs get stiff. Rub molasses on legs make stiffness not so bad. Molasses stick legs bottom of canoe. Molasses not much good for stiff legs, but my ancestors think so; not their fault, just mistake; they not know molasses good to eat.

Squamish elder Louis Miranda also shared stories of Vancouver's visit in *From Maps to Metaphors: The Pacific World of George Vancouver.* The Squamish people believed initially that the white-skinned men were from the land of the dead, and the smoke coming from their mouths (from their pipes) showed that they were eating fire. After the ships had departed, the Squamish people named the site Whul-whul-LAY-ton which means "Whiteman Place."

Leaving the natives that day, the two ships continued along the western shore, passing several small islands. The sailors were unable to obtain soundings at many locations due to the great depth of the water. Vancouver's journal did not mention naming the islands in the sound, but his chartmaker showed them as "Jarvis's Isles." He landed for the night near the western point of the entrance to the Sound, which he named Point Gower after the British Captain (later Admiral) Sir Erasmus Gower, although the expedition's charts showed "Gore Point." Finally he named the entire waterway—"which I distinguished by the name of Howe's Sound, in honor of Admiral Earl Howe."

The following day, Saturday, they left Point Gower at 4 a.m. and continued north in their small boats along the eastern shore of the Gulph of Georgia, surveying and naming geographical features. The boats returned south in late June, and Vancouver met the Spanish explorers Galiano and Valdes off Point Grey. To his dismay, Vancouver found that the Spaniards had already named Howe's Sound and the Gulph of Georgia. Although he usually recognized place names given by other explorers, he decided to retain the English names because he had claimed the Gulph for England.

Vancouver's surveys were a crucial factor in maintaining British title to parts of the west coast, and the British Admiralty used the details shown on his charts. Sadly, despite the many times that he interacted with native people, he almost completely ignored the traditional names with which they had endowed their territories.

At last, during this year of 1792, most of Europe was becoming aware that the western coast of Canada was an area of primordial beauty and potential riches. Howe Sound and the Squamish Valley were a small but breathtakingly beautiful part, still generally unknown. At this time, eastern Canada was already settled and involved in commercial enterprises—the Hudson's Bay Company had been trading for over 100 years, and Nova Scotia, New Brunswick, Prince Edward Island and Quebec were settled provinces (Nova Scotia had a population of 17,000 by 1775). The west coast needed a financial attraction to draw settlers. The first commercial excitement, however, was of the type that typically did not encourage settlement.

In 1778, when Captain James Cook had visited the west coast of Vancouver Island, his crew unknowingly uncovered a product that would become an irresistible attraction for traders. The natives had bartered the skins of the sea otter for metal and other rather valueless items. When Cook's ships reached China on the journey home, the sailors were astonished at the enthusiasm of the Chinese merchants for the skins. In fact, the demand was so great, and the prices paid so high, that Cook's lieutenant King wrote, "The rage with which our seamen were possessed to return [for more trading] . . . was not far short of mutiny."[6] Captain Cook quickly realized the future economic potential and included in his journal a plan for fur trading between the coast of North America and China. He did not publish this plan until 1784. Immediately afterwards, in 1785, traders began sailing for the Pacific coast to tap the first of its newly-discovered riches—sea otter pelts.

By 1801, at the height of the excitement, the coastal natives as far north as Alaska traded with approximately 23 ships.[7] Still, the islands masking Sea to Sky Country discouraged all but two or three traders from extending their search into the waiting waters.[8] Few white men visited Howe Sound for the next 50 years, until the lure of gold attracted prospectors and surveyors.

CHAPTER 3

THE SEARCHERS

Not only Fraser's River and its tributary streams, but also the whole country situated to the eastward of the Gulf of Georgia, as far north as Johnstone's Straits, is one continued bed of gold of incalculable value and extent.

—Governor James Douglas, 1859

G old fever. Close to $50 million worth of gold was taken out of British Columbia in 1858. Over 30,000 gold miners flooded into the colony. During the previous two years, word had gradually spread about gold finds near the junction of the Thompson and Fraser Rivers, but when Governor Douglas allegedly shipped 800 ounces of gold to the mint in San Francisco in February 1858, the word spread like wildfire.[1]

Gold not only replaced fur-trading as the prime source of interest for those looking for a good income; it brought potential settlers who could develop the land and increase commerce. The British Parliament decided that the colony now required a formal government to establish laws for the growing population and the new set of problems associated with it.

James Douglas, who had been governor of Vancouver Island since 1851, now became the first governor of the new and separate Crown Colony of British Columbia on November 19, 1858.

VICTORIA GAZETTE, November 25, 1858 Page 1

LETTER FROM NEW FORT LANGLEY

INSTALLATION OF THE GOVERNMENT OF BRITISH COLUMBIA

NEW FORT LANGLEY, 20 NOV. 1858

Editors Gazette: Yesterday, the birthday of British Columbia, was ushered in by a steady rain, which continued perseveringly throughout the whole day, and in a great measure marred the solemnity of the proclamation of the Colony. His Excellency Governor Douglas [and other officials] proceeded . . . to New Fort Langley, where preparations were made for the ceremonial of the following day.

On Friday morning, the 19th inst., His Excellency accompanied by his suite, and received by a guard of honor commanded by Capt. Grant, proceeded up the steep bank which leads to the palisade. Arrived there, a salute of eighteen guns commenced pealing from the Beaver [ship], awakening all the echoes of the opposite mountains. In another moment the flag of Britain was floating, or, to speak the truth, dripping over the principal entrance . . . On leaving the Fort . . . another salute of 17 guns was fired from the battlements with even a grander effect than the salute of the previous day.

The boundaries established by the Act of July 28, 1863, were the same as today's provincial boundaries except that Vancouver Island was a separate colony until August 1866.

Squamish River Gold Rush

If gold fever raced up the Fraser River with a roar, it crept up the Squamish River with a whisper.

In dispatches asking the British Parliament for aid to enforce laws and build roads and bridges for the growing colony, Governor Douglas reported several instances of gold found on the shores of Howe Sound, mostly by Squamish natives. One purse of gold dust brought to his attention in 1858 contained about 20 English pounds worth of the metal.[2] This was at a time when a Fraser River miner could pan hundreds of dollars worth in one day. Nevertheless, for "one bit" (12 1/2 cents per copy), potential gold seekers could read enough in the Victoria *Gazette* to fuel their enthusiasm for a possible gold strike that might equal the one on the Fraser.

In October 1858, the newspaper reported that prospectors had uncovered gold on the Squamish River from as far back as 1856. Several men followed the lure of riches and explored the southern section of the river bed. The natives fired their fever by telling them about quantities of gold farther up the river. One prospector, a Mr. Redmond, persevered in the Squamish Valley's south end, close to Howe Sound, returning to his base in Point Roberts with about 80 cents worth of dust which he had found in three pans of dirt.

His discovery was enough to inspire groups of prospectors to purchase supplies and set out for the lower Squamish. One man returned with the news that he could make seven to eight dollars a day from the river. The enthusiasts returned to the area and used native guides, who were very friendly and helpful. According to the reports, they trekked 96 kilometres (60 miles) up the river, prospecting several bars along the way and finding about 50 cents worth of gold to the pan.

The *Gazette* printed a series of articles between October 7 and 19, 1858, featuring reports and letters from prospectors who had been successful on the Squamish. On October 16, however, the editor warned, "It is to be distinctly understood that none of the gentlemen engaged in these undertakings . . . are personally known to us," and cautioned that it would be best for anyone interested to wait for more definite and positive information.

Returning to Point Roberts, the prospectors gathered provisions for a winter camp and wrote about their finds to the editor of the *Gazette* on October 19. They also stipulated, "Please advise any person coming up the river to avoid bringing liquor of any description."

Evidently, from the lack of further news bulletins, no wild rush followed.

Overland to the Cariboo

The area was viewed as a possible gateway to the Cariboo gold fields, however, and that same fall of 1858, Governor Douglas dispatched an expedition to explore the Squamish Valley for a more practicable route to the interior. The existing routes—one following the treacherous canyons of the Fraser River and the other involving the difficult portages between Harrison and Lillooet—were both arduous and dangerous. Hudson's Bay Company chief trader Joseph W. McKay, a very active young fellow, full of vigour and intelligence,[3] was 29 years old that September when, accompanied by a veteran California miner named William Downie as well as four Canadians and three native guides, he led the expedition from Port Pemberton on Lillooet Lake to the south, following the Cheakamus and Squamish Rivers to Howe Sound. They were the first white men to pass the body of water now named Alta Lake, near

Whistler Mountain, and just south of there McKay named Daisy Lake, impressed with its amazingly green water. He did not mention whether he named it for the flowers or a particular lady.[4]

He noted the lake had been formed by a great rockslide which dammed the Cheakamus River and flooded the forested land for 5 kilometres (3 miles) around. Dead trees were still standing in the water. The native people reported that part of The Barrier's lava face had crumbled and roared down into the valley only three years earlier, in 1855. After the men had passed the slide area, they climbed the rugged hills just to the south and were the first white men to view the devastation from above.

McKay's experience with the Squamish natives was not as amicable as Captain Vancouver's. After he received a warning that they planned to kill his native guides, he learned they were at war with all the neighbouring tribes. Desperate for provisions, but unable to attain any from the unfriendly natives, his group purchased two small canoes and left the mouth of the Squamish River late at night. After a long paddle south through Howe Sound in the dark, they were thankful to reach Gower Point at the southwest point of the sound early the next morning.

McKay decided that the route could be used as an alternative to the gold fields in the Cariboo. With proper engineering, it could be suitable for a mule trail, the lack of soil being the greatest disadvantage. In his report to Governor Douglas in October 1858, McKay described the riches of the "Bottoms of the Skow-komish" (Squamish River valley), which had taken them six days to reach. He said that the valley was well timbered, mainly with huge Douglas firs, which could be used for the largest spars, a profitable commercial product used on sailing ships. Cedars were also abundant, and the land appeared well able to support farming.[5]

Two years later, in 1860, gold again drew men into a search, this time a second look for another route to the interior. Richard Mayne, a spirited young naval lieutenant,[6] endured repeated hardships investigating a route from Jervis Inlet. This was several kilometres north of Howe Sound, and William Downie had already reported two years earlier in *Hunting for Gold: Reminiscences of Personal Experience* that the route was not feasible. Nevertheless, Mayne received orders to attempt to find a valley which could be the site of a road from the head of Jervis Inlet to the Upper Fraser River near Chilcotin. In his detailed diary (later published as *Four Years in British Columbia and Vancouver Island*), Mayne called this "the most arduous trip I made in British Columbia."

Lava cliff called The Barrier, formed thousands of years ago when hot lava from Mount Garibaldi poured down between the mountain and the edge of the glacier. Garibaldi Lake can be seen in the background, covered with snow. *(UBC/Spils)*

Mayne provided such a clear description of his travelling equipment that one can picture him vividly, toiling along the trails with his native guides. He wore a shooting jacket with several pockets, and durable corduroy trousers, tied under the knee "after the fashion of English navvies," to support their weight when wet. He wore an old uniform cap to impress the natives who assumed that the wearer held the position of a great chief. He slung an aneroid barometer over his shoulder and carried a spy-glass. In a small valise, his extra clothing consisted of a flannel shirt, several pairs of socks, and a Hudson's Bay blue frock coat with a hood and gold lace on the cuffs, which he wore on important visits with the natives. He slept in a coat and pants made of blue blanket material, an early version of a sleeping bag.

His porters dressed in a similar manner to the Europeans, in trousers and shirts, and each carried an old coat to wear in town. They travelled barefoot or wrapped pieces of deerskin around their feet. They usually

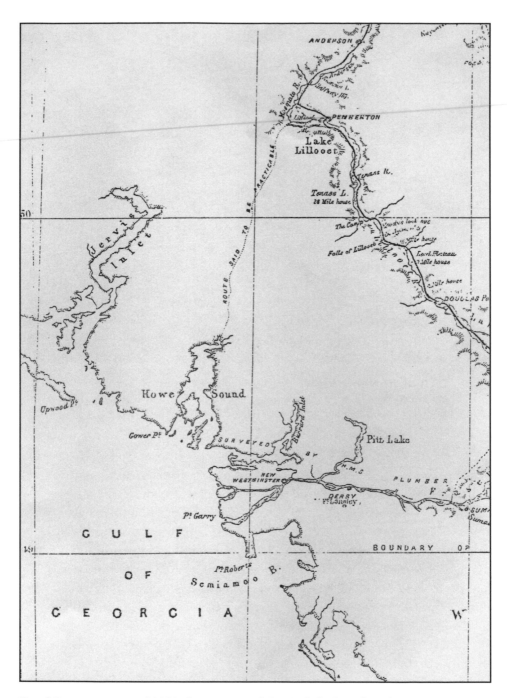

Royal Engineers map of 1859 showing Joseph McKay's finding that there was a "practicable route" for an overland passage from Howe Sound north to the gold fields. The HMS *Plumper* carried out the survey. *(BCARS)*

asked for shoes at the beginning of the trip, but carried them in their backpacks.

For food, the men depended upon bacon, flour, tea and coffee, and a bottle of brandy "in case of accidents."

Having left the ship, Mayne and Dr. Wood, the ship's surgeon, with five Sechelt and Loquilt natives, slogged through impenetrable bush and flooded mountain rivers for two days, finally reaching an impassable morass. Exhausted, they returned to Jervis Inlet.

The natives, in their enthusiasm to end the tortuous journey, told Mayne that they knew a way to cross from Jervis Inlet to Howe Sound and from there up the Squamish and Cheakamus Rivers to Port Pemberton on Lillooet Lake, a part of the Harrison–Lillooet Trail.

This was basically the same route McKay's expedition followed in 1858, but Mayne was to travel it from south to north. The men could have begun, with much less exhaustion, by taking a boat to the northern shore of Howe Sound. Instead, they first crossed a ridge of the Coast Mountains, a route of no use for any practical purpose.

They took three days to descend to the Squamish River, which they crossed about 16 kilometres (10 miles) north of Howe Sound. Their average speed was little more than a kilometre an hour through knee-deep swamp, moss-slicked rock, thick bush and incessant mosquitoes. This hardship was too much for Dr. Wood, and he left the group to travel back to New Westminster by canoe with some Squamish natives. The impossibility of their mission is reflected in the fact that no road exists in that area across the mountains to this day.

Richard Mayne's group visited the Squamish village, named Elawho, then camped farther up the river for the night, just north of the settlement. Mayne described the arable land and rich soil situated between the two rivers, the "Tseearkamisht" [Cheakamus] and the "Squawmisht" [Squamish]. He believed that sternwheelers could travel for several kilometres up the Squamish River, but the mouth of the Cheakamus was too silted up for ships to enter. The men passed several villages along the river where the natives were fishing for salmon. They met the chief of these villages, who reported that his people also grew potatoes in several of the valley clearings. He also told them the Squamish had not made a trail from the villages to Howe Sound, as they always travelled that route by canoe.

The party followed the ridges and streams through the Cheakamus

Canyon to Daisy Lake, camped for the night, and saw for themselves the results of the gigantic landslide from The Barrier that formed Daisy Lake and dammed the river, as reported by McKay two years earlier. Mayne remarked on the dead trees standing in about two metres (six feet) of water, which looked as though it had receded from its original depth. The trees were fire-charred and blackened by this time, probably as a result of forest fires. About eight kilometres (five miles) northeast of the flooded area, the travellers reached a lake where they stopped for breakfast, relaxing on the grass in the shade of a tree. Mayne wrote, "Finding the Indians knew no name for it, I called it Green Lake, from the remarkably green colour of the water."

Their trek followed well-used native trails north towards Port Pemberton, but there were still hardships. One night a torrential thunderstorm terrorized the natives, and the mosquitoes were the worst that Mayne had ever experienced in British Columbia. He hung a mosquito net on crossed sticks, making a small tent-like structure, and tucked it around himself when he sat inside. He also had brought a head-bag made of crepe. This consisted of a long veil fastened to the crown of his straw hat and tied around the neck. He inserted small cane hoops into the veil to hold it away from his face and keep the ravenous mosquitoes from settling on the veil and biting him through it. The natives coated themselves with oil and mud, but still suffered greatly.

Mayne's final report on the feasibility of road construction from Howe Sound to Port Pemberton paralleled McKay's—it could be done, but it was not practicable to build another route to the gold fields so near the Port Douglas-Lillooet Lake trail. The idea of a wagon road from the head of Jervis Inlet to the Fraser River in the Cariboo went no further.

The frantic rush for gold sparked dreams of riches from other hidden minerals, and Howe Sound disclosed its earliest lode. At White Cliff Point, north of Burrard Inlet on Howe Sound's eastern shore, a discovery of copper ore in 1865 caused ripples of excitement to extend even to Governor Douglas. A group of investors formed a company named the Howe Sound Copper Mines Ltd. With the assistance of the governor, who loaned his steam yacht for the visit, the company brought an expert, Legh Harnett, to give his opinion on the mine's potential worth. Mr. Harnett pronounced it "by far the best thing of the kind discovered in the Colony, and quite as legitimate as any on the Pacific Coast." His glowing report (published as *Two Lectures on British Columbia*), plus the results of further drilling, encouraged the company to apply for a prospecting licence in March 1870 to cover 186 hectares (460 acres). The assistant commissioner of Lands and Works in Victoria approved it immediately.[7]

Although the mine produced successfully for some time, lack of capital caused its eventual abandonment.[8] The reality went the way of many prospectors' dreams, although not too far north of this location, a major copper lode at Britannia Mountain was waiting to be discovered at the turn of the century.

CHAPTER 4

THE SETTING

*Preliminary to our arrival our Indian canoe-men, who are in
highest spirits, brought our two remaining canoes in line, and,
keeping slow stroke in unison, sang an agreeable but rather plaintive
chorus in admirable time—reminding some of us of bygone days when
the more lively paddle-song of the French Canadian voyageurs was a
familiar song.*

—from the diary of A.C. Anderson, Indian reserves
commissioner, on his trip up the Squamish valley to
establish Indian reserves, November 25, 1876

British Columbia was a Crown Colony with its own government.
Victoria was thriving and the first sawmills on Vancouver
Island were sending their harsh screams throughout the community. The population was expanding, and the British Royal Engineers
were busy planning and building trails and roads. Governor Douglas was
involved in plans to establish the capital of British Columbia at New
Westminster. Howe Sound and the Squamish Valley echoed to the activities of a few gold seekers and the daily activities of the Squamish people.

In 1859, for the first time in many years, a large ship sailed into Howe
Sound waters. The HMS *Plumper*, a man-of-war, was under the command
of Captain George Richards, 39 years old and rather a small man physically, but a mass of shrewdness and humour.[1] He undertook the first survey of the sound and its islands since Captain Vancouver had visited in
1792.

White settlers had not yet discovered the surrounding lands and
would certainly be discouraged from taking up residence there after reading Captain Richards' negative report of 1864. He characterized Howe
Sound as a useless sheet of water with few anchorages, as precipitous
mountains rose abruptly from the edge of the water.[2] He stated that no
available land existed for settlers, and the Squamish River was useless for

A drawing which appeared in the *Illustrated London News*, 1862. The British survey ship HMS *Plumper* charted the islands and shores throughout Howe Sound in 1859. Its captain, George Richards, considered the sound a useless sheet of water with no anchorages and no room for settlers. *(CVA OUT P1097.638)*

boats to enter the country's interior. Richards was obviously not aware of the reports Joseph McKay and Richard Mayne wrote after their overland explorations, in which they suggested that the Squamish Valley was suitable for farming.

Captain Vancouver had named Howe Sound after Admiral Howe (later the Right Honourable Richard Scrope, Lord Howe), who was the British hero of the "Glorious First of June" battle in 1794. Following this lead, Captain Richards named several islands for admirals—Bowen, Bowyer, Gambier and Keats—who had fought in that famous encounter in which the British defeated a superior French fleet.

He designated Atkinson Point the eastern entrance to the sound, and Gower Point, nearly 19 kilometres (11 miles) away, the western boundary. For sailors entering Howe Sound from the west, he pointed out that Bowen Island was an important navigational aid as its round summit rose to nearly 762 metres (2479 feet) and indicated the entrance to the sound from all directions.

For seafarers coming from the north and planning to enter the Fraser

River, Richards recommended they set a bearing on a line between Passage Island and the peak on Anvil Island in order to clear the edge of shallow Sturgeon Bank. He also recommended Port Graves, the most easterly of the three bays on southern Gambier Island, as the main anchorage in Howe Sound, although its entrance was not apparent until passing Hope Point on the bay's eastern shore.

He had previously, in 1856, changed the "Gulf" to the "Strait" of Georgia, after surveys showed that, in fact, an exit existed from the Gulf of Georgia north of Vancouver Island. But even today, some long-time residents still refer to it as "The Gulf."[3]

Howe Sound was ready, well named, well charted, a stage well set. And soon a new cast of actors would enter the scene.

Early Industry

Governor Douglas issued the first Land Proclamation in 1859 to regulate land claims on Crown land in British Columbia. He established that the land must have been surveyed and would be sold at public auction for 10 shillings per acre. One year later, on January 4, 1860, a more detailed proclamation stated that British subjects, and aliens who took an oath of allegiance, could acquire unoccupied and unsurveyed land. Potential settlers could register their claims of up to 64.8 hectares (160 acres) by providing the best possible description and a rough plan of the lot to a magistrate with a fee of 8 shillings. Once the land had been formally surveyed, they could purchase it for 10 shillings per acre, but they had to occupy it continuously and make permanent improvements worth 10 shillings per acre. Douglas's Country Land Act of 1861 made purchase even easier by lowering the price to 4 shillings and 2 pence per acre.

The first settlers on the future site of the city of Vancouver were the earliest to apply the land proclamation in that area. John Morton, Samuel Brighouse and William Hailstone together claimed 222.5 hectares (550 acres) in 1862, bounded by today's Stanley Park and Burrard Street, English Bay and Burrard Inlet.[4]

In the summer of the next year, T.W. Graham and Co. pre-empted 194 hectares (480 acres) for logging on the north shore of Burrard Inlet, just east of the present Lonsdale Avenue. The finest and most easily accessible timber surrounded Graham's new Pioneer Mills. It was sawing 12,192 metres (40,000 feet) of lumber a day by the end of 1863, but the isolated location, delays and expenses forced the company to put the mill up for auction. John Oscar Smith bought it in December 1863, but had to auction it in 1864 to pay off the mortgage. Sewell (Sue) Moody bought the mill and improved and expanded it to a successful enterprise.[5]

While loggers felled thousands of trees around Burrard Inlet, the eyes of the sawmill owners naturally turned westward, to the untouched stands of old-growth giants around Howe Sound. Moody's Mill on the north shore and Hastings Mill on the south side of Burrard Inlet sent the first loggers to the shores and islands of Howe Sound and the hillsides of the Squamish Valley. As early as 1865, Hastings Sawmill leased the timber rights on hundreds of hectares near Gibsons and on the south side of Gambier Island. In 1870, Moody leased land on the Squamish River near the confluence of the Cheakamus River, and also at Point Atkinson.[6]

Loggers, then, were probably among the first white men to break the long silence and change the wilderness landscape revered by the native inhabitants. According to pre-emption records, three men claimed 64.8 hectares (160 acres) each on Howe Sound in 1872, 80 years after Captain Vancouver's visit: January 8, William J. Challenger, on Anvil Island; March 25, Joseph Silvia Seamers, Howe Sound; May 28, Ira Furry, on Bowen Island. Their occupations were not listed. Two years later, in July 1874, William Challenger was listed as a farmer, probably the first on Anvil Island.

The Voters' List dated September 2, 1875, showed nine residents on Howe Sound, all "lumbermen." One of them was Ira Furry, the brother of Oliver Furry who would play an important part in the initial copper mining development at Britannia in the early 1900s. For the next few years, the New Westminster District Voters' List showed mostly lumbermen as Howe Sound residents. In fact, before the first settlers had arrived at Gibson's Landing in 1885, loggers had removed most of the trees at the site.[7]

Besides farming and logging, a small fishing industry was making its mark on one of the islands. A group of whalers, who in 1868 established a camp on Pasley Island, just west of Bowen Island, took advantage of the passing pods of whales in the Strait of Georgia. They towed their catches to almost the same shores as the natives, who had caught whales there for generations and left the bleached skeletons to dot Pasley Island's eastern beach for many years.[8] August Jack Khahtsahlano recounted one story which explained that when the white men first visited Bowen Island, they found the beaches dotted with white bones and therefore

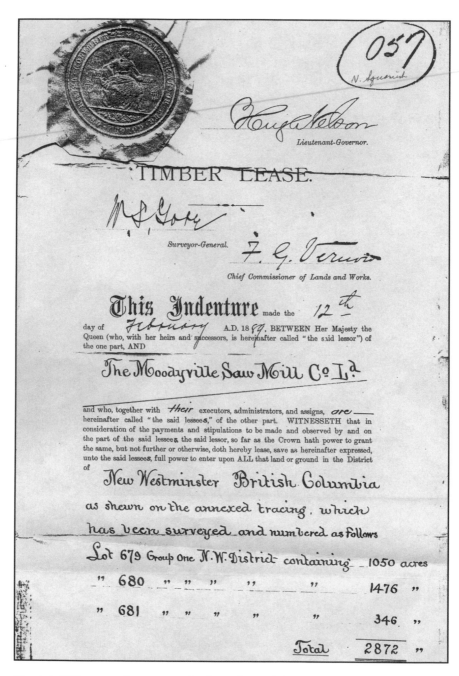

Hugh Nelson

Lieutenant-Governor.

TIMBER LEASE.

M.S. Gore

Surveyor-General.

F. G. Vernon

Chief Commissioner of Lands and Works.

This Indenture made the 12ᵗʰ day of *February* A.D. 18*87*, BETWEEN Her Majesty the Queen (who, with her heirs and successors, is hereinafter called "the said lessor") of the one part, AND

The Moodyville Saw Mill Co Ld

and who, together with *their* executors, administrators, and assigns, *are* hereinafter called "the said lessees," of the other part. WITNESSETH that in consideration of the payments and stipulations to be made and observed by and on the part of the said lessees, the said lessor, so far as the Crown hath power to grant the same, but not further or otherwise, doth hereby lease, save as hereinafter expressed, unto the said lessees, full power to enter upon ALL that land or ground in the District of

New Westminster British Columbia as shewn on the annexed tracing, which has been surveyed and numbered as follows

Lot 679 Group One N.W. District containing	1050 acres
" 680 " " " " "	1476 "
" 681 " " " " "	346 "
Total	2872 "

Moody's Mill, near what is now the foot of Lonsdale Avenue in North Vancouver, took out timber leases on Crown land along Howe Sound's shores and islands and in the Squamish Valley. Hastings Mill, on the south shore of Burrard Inlet, also sent loggers to cut the magnificent firs and cedars. *(DA)*

called it "Bone Island." Later settlers called Pasley and Worlcombe "the Whale Islands."

Joseph Silvey, Peter Smith and Harry Trim, a former gold miner, made their living from whaling in the sound for several years. The 1874 Voters' List showed James and Harry Trim as fishermen on Pasley Island. Joseph Silvey and Peter Smith were registered at Granville (now Vancouver). The men built small cabins on the island for their native wives, and on April 1, 1872, Josephine Silvey was born there, probably the first child of European heritage born on Howe Sound.

In a 1943 interview with Major J.S. Matthews of the Vancouver Archives, Josephine's younger sister, Mrs. James Walker, recalled the excitement in the busy little settlement when the whalers towed the huge mammals to shore. The first person to sight the sails of the schooner towing the whale called out, and the families ran to the shore and watched the whale's white belly, then its black back, as it twisted and turned in the waves.

With the schooner tied up to a small wharf, the men slowly hauled the whale up the shore with a thick cable attached to a man-powered windlass. They used large knives to cut the carcass into pieces about 30 centimetres (12 inches) thick, then boiled the pieces in large pots under the roof of a small shed to extract the valuable oil.

The Pemberton Trail

While Howe Sound was welcoming a gradually increasing number of white men, the politicians were making history. On July 20, 1871, British Columbia joined Confederation and became a province of the Dominion of Canada.

One clause of the Confederation agreement again brought surveyors to the Squamish Valley and northwards. The construction of a trans-Canada railway was to begin within two years of the date of union. The promise of an overland route for settlers caused almost as much excitement as the decision about which location would be its western terminus. Land speculators were buying up lots around the Port Moody and Granville waterfronts, while the Canadian government was sending out surveyors to find the best route to the coast.

In 1873, Marcus Smith, a surveyor in charge of Canadian Pacific Railway surveys for British Columbia, led a team north from Howe Sound, past Daisy and Green Lakes, to Pemberton and Lillooet. The government was considering the Squamish Valley as one possible route among several, with a terminus on Burrard Inlet. Smith's crew pushed a trail through as directly as possible, with no concern for ease of travel. This rough line, never designed for permanent use, climbed up and down hills and around rocky projections. Eventually Vancouver became the Canadian Pacific Railway terminus, with the tracks reaching the city through the lower Fraser Valley, but the Pacific Great Eastern Railway did follow this Squamish Valley route forty years later.

The influx of loggers and settlers to Granville, and the growing population on Vancouver Island and in New Westminster, provided a ready market not only for whale fat, used for lamps and machinery, but also, more importantly, for meat to feed the logging crews. By the early 1870s, the Cariboo ranchers were ready and eager to supply beef to the receptive communities. The British *Colonist*, Victoria's newspaper (also called the Victoria *Colonist*), reported on June 28, 1872: "The large stock-farming interests of the interior are paralysed for want of such an outlet; and the large communities on the seaboard are, from the same cause, consuming foreign beef in payment of which the country is being drained of its wealth at the rate of something like $125,000 a year."

How to get the cattle from their ranges to the coastal markets was a problem not easily solved. As early as 1861, Dr. John S. Helmcken, a member of the British Columbia legislature, had proposed a trail from Lillooet south through the Squamish Valley to Howe Sound, then east over the mountains to Burrard Inlet. Marcus Smith's railway survey trail served as the rough beginnings of a route to Howe Sound. Smith had not planned to have it used in this way, and the ruggedness of its path caused problems for the cattle trail.

In 1873, William Sampson, the job foreman (paid $100 per month by the provincial government), examined the passes and valleys and gave his assessment of the route: "a good cattle trail could be constructed the whole distance from the Pemberton Meadows to Burrard Inlet for $8,000.00."[9]

Although the trail's construction commenced in 1873 near Lillooet, severe problems developed and progress was slow. In 1875, work began at both ends of the trail, one gang building from Pemberton south to Howe Sound, and the other starting at Burrard Inlet near Lynn Creek and working north up Seymour Creek.

George Jenkinson, the superintendent in charge of the Burrard Inlet

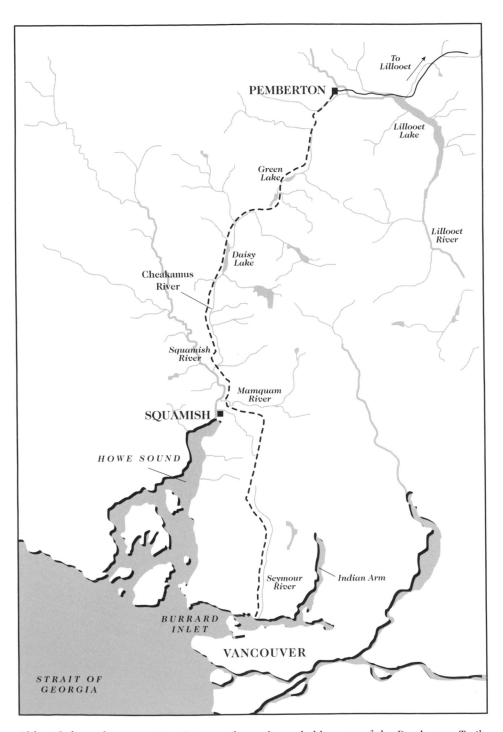

Although few references exist, this map shows the probable route of the Pemberton Trail.

northbound route, sent a report to Victoria in which he described some of the problems that thoroughly discouraged his men. "We managed to get along very well as long as the dry weather lasted, but about the middle of September the rains set in, and then our difficulty commenced. We had then 26 miles of trail completed; we had struck a beaver swamp which would have supplied us with horse feed for some time in dry weather. I tied the horses there one night on what was dry ground, and in the morning we found them standing in water up to their bellies in a lake. We had to wade up to the knees to get them out; we had to send them off to the Coast to save their lives."

After attempting to work in the rain and mud for twelve more days, they realized that they were making no headway so decided to stop for the season.

The southbound trail progressed at a reasonable rate, but had its own set of problems. When the crew reached the rockslide at The Barrier, just north of Mount Garibaldi, they had to construct bridges from rock to rock, remove some of the boulders with levers, and fill the holes between the rocks with decayed wood because of the lack of soil. The trail through the slide area, a distance of about 300 metres (1000 feet), took them a week to complete.

Water was also the crew's adversary. From the mouth of the Squamish River at the north end of Howe Sound, east to the mountains, heavy rains inundated the sandy plain and marooned the men for three days. They then attempted to cross to higher ground and packed their horses with supplies, but the animals sank into the sand. Eventually the men clambered over fallen trees with the supplies on their own backs.

The British Columbia Public Works, Bridges, Roads and Buildings Department had commissioned a competent engineer to survey the entire route, and in 1876 he encouraged work to continue as he felt the plan was practical. The foreman of the job, A.J. McLellan, disagreed and notified the chief commissioner of Public Works that the trail should end at Howe Sound, eliminating the extra 68 kilometres (42 miles) across the mountains to Burrard Inlet. There was little fodder for cattle on this portion of the trail, and the steep grades and marshy land would make the upkeep very difficult. However, the demand for cattle influenced the government's decision and construction continued.

McLellan's report was prophetic. Only one herd of cattle ever made the trip from the Cariboo to Burrard Inlet. In the fall of 1877, Robert

Carson of the then well-known Pavilion Mountain Ranch (sometimes referred to as Carson's Kingdom), and Richard Hoey, both ranchers, and a native named Pecullah Kosta, herded 200 head to the coast. The only major problem in reaching Howe Sound was the steep section above the Cheakamus Canyon, but the conditions to Burrard Inlet became a nightmare, with almost no feed and the trail a sea of mud. They arrived with emaciated animals. George Black, one of the first butchers to set up shop in Granville, bought the healthiest, and the rest had to fatten up over the winter for market.[10]

The trail from Howe Sound to Burrard Inlet fell into disuse and became choked with fallen trees and fresh growth. The whole project had cost about $40,000 to construct.

The Pemberton to Howe Sound section survived and became the first direct connection between the two points, although a rugged one. An early Pemberton resident described it as a "heartbreaker, built so that it climbed up and down most of the ridges between Pemberton and Squamish."[11] Later the government upgraded it to a wagon road, but about 80 years were to pass before a surfaced road replaced it. Even now, segments of the old trail are still visible.

Native Land Boundaries

Britain developed a colonial policy of setting aside land in reservations for native people to live on, and by 1876 the Dominion government had appointed three Indian reserves commissioners to specify native land boundaries in British Columbia and prevent future Indian land disputes. To complete this task, white men once more travelled through the Squamish Valley. On Tuesday, November 21, a fine day, Alexander Caulfield Anderson, one of the commissioners, and his team set out in three canoes to ascend the Squamish River. With the assistance of Chief Joseph, they laid out dimensions for the reservations.

They reached the uppermost inhabited village, Skow-a-shin, on November 23, and Anderson's meticulously detailed diary (now in the BC Archives) contains one of the few descriptions of Squamish villages written at that time:

The country here is densely wooded: but the few patches that have been cleared by the natives around the village exhibit a prolific soil, and yield, by their account, good returns of the few vegetables cultivated, chiefly potatoes. The Indians value this point for the fine timber (Red Cedar = Thuja Gigantea) which it produces, and which to them is important for the making of canoes. Accordingly we laid off for them a tract, as indicated by themselves, extending from the River bank to the Mountain-base. We also gave them two Cedar posts to place at as many ancient burial grounds. The first of these, marked "Indian Grave-yard," and distinguished by a single circle at the head, with a Cross at the back of the Post, is to be placed at Pooy-awm, on the left bank, about 7 ms [11 km] above and North of Skowashin. The second, similarly marked, but distinguished by two circles, is to be placed at Chuk-chuk, on the right bank, about midway between Skowashin and Pooy-awm.

They delineated several more sites, including See-o-chum, Kow-tain and Euk-quat-sum (where Chief Paul resided), which reached from "Sta-a-mis Island northward to include the bend and low island above the village."

The men worked in an almost constant heavy downpour. Anderson's diary entry for Monday, November 27, reads:

Sharp frost last night. Strong Westerly gale during the day—some rain and snow—in all a very disagreeable day. Busily occupied till late at night completing details of our assignments to the Indians this quarter, writing letters etc. Before retiring for the night I, on part of the Commission, addressed the Indians who were assembled for a parting interview around our principal camp fire. Response made by Joseph and another expressing the satisfaction of the Indians in every respect of the action of the Commission, and repeating their assurances of loyalty to the Queen and their determination to strive for improvement in all conditions of life under the instruction given to them.

The next morning, after an apparently successful mission, they left on their ship *Leonora* for Sechelt. On the way they stopped on the west shore of Howe Sound at a point called Ka-ak-ul-tun, opposite Woolridge Island, staked a fishing and hunting station of approximately 162 hectares (400 acres), and marked the adjacent burial ground. An hour later they also visited Sch-unk, opposite Keats Island, where they found an old woman as sole occupant at the time.

In a period of less than twenty years, English names identified Howe

Sound features, logging had moved into its forests, a trail from Squamish opened up contact with the Pemberton–Lillooet region, and the Squamish people lived with boundaries outlining their lands.

CHAPTER 5

THE SETTLERS

My father built a log house . . . The house had one doorway, no
opening for windows. The first night our door was a piece of carpet.
My mother told me, in later years, that the first thing she did was to
sit down on a pile of bedding and cry bitterly.

—recalled by Bessie Galbraith McIntosh, who
arrived on Bowen Island in 1899 at the age of ten

Washed by the same waves that crashed against the craggy promontory of Point Atkinson a short distance away, a small group of rocky islets echoed to the surge and ebb of the tide and the cries of an eagle perched high in a solitary tree. He was the only resident, except for those in their graves below. The Grebe Islets, as they were later known, were the final resting place for many Squamish people, laid there reverently under cedar slabs by their families. "Dead Watch Tree"[1] marked their burial ground for many years, while an increasing number of ships passed just south of the isolated rocks, and commerce expanded in the nearby towns of Moodyville and Granville.

The ships came to take the magnificent timber from the shores of Burrard Inlet. Gigantic spars were shipped to Scotland, France, Australia, China and other parts of the world. The government of the fledgling Dominion of Canada recognized Burrard Inlet's potential as a port and the need for a beacon to guide these ships in and out of the harbour. The Department of Marine and Fisheries decided on Point Atkinson as the location for the first lighthouse on the inlet, rather than small, rocky Passage Island, their initial choice.

In 1872, a builder named Arthur Finney received the approval of the Marine Department to build the lighthouse for a fee of $4250. Although preparations moved slowly, and he did not set out from Nanaimo with his construction crew until May 1874, they completed the building by June 10.[2]

The first lighthouse was a frame house with a wooden tower on the roof. At a height of 27.5 metres (90 feet) above sea level, the light was visible as far as 22.5 kilometres (14 miles) distant. Opening celebrations were postponed because the wrong type of light arrived from England, and a replacement took six more months to be delivered and installed.

Eventually, on March 17, 1875, Edwin Woodward, appointed light-keeper with a salary of $800 per year, arrived with his wife Ann and their two children to make the new landmark their home. They were probably the first white family to live on Howe Sound. Standing on the spray-washed rocks guarding their solitary residence, they could enjoy breath-taking views of the green Howe Sound islands, the rolling expanse of the Strait of Georgia, the tree-clad slopes of Kitsilano and Point Grey, and the narrow entrance to Burrard Inlet's inner harbour. Beauty, however, could not compete with isolation and loneliness.

Although Moodyville and Granville were reasonably close, travel from the lighthouse was difficult. When her husband made one of his rare visits to the townsites by boat, Ann Woodward had to stay to tend the light. The first white woman to live in what is now West Vancouver, she bore her third child, James Atkinson, the following April without medical assistance. She had no female companionship and saw only one woman, a Squamish native, during her entire stay.[3]

The crew of the government steamer *Sir James Douglas*, that

The original Point Atkinson lighthouse was built in 1874. This photo was taken c. 1910. *(CVA OUT P420 N140)*

Captain White, of the tug *Etta White*, was one of those who transported settlers to their new homes around Howe Sound and delivered their mail and supplies. Often ships' captains and crews were the only human beings the loggers and pioneers saw for weeks at a time. *(Vancouver Maritime Museum)*

stopped occasionally with supplies, and Captain White of the tug *Etta White* were virtually the only source of human contact for the family. A high point of excitement was the delivery of a cow by tugboat. Dropped overboard, the animal was hauled to shore by a line tied around its horns. With mooing and expletives filling the air, the Woodwards managed to pull it up the trail to its new home.

Deer meat and a vegetable garden supplied most of the family's needs, except the need for companionship. This lack eventually led to the Woodwards leaving their isolated home for Ontario in 1879.

In 1939, Hiram Woodward, their eldest child, was interviewed by Major J.S. Matthews of the Vancouver Archives and recounted memories of their departure and the takeover by the new lightkeeper, R.G. Wellwood:

My sister visited Point Atkinson before they left there to return to Ontario. She told me Mr. Wellwood would only give her [mother] five dollars for the cow, and, of course, she could not sell it to anyone else, anyway. And Mrs. Wellwood would only give her two bits [25 cents] for the down pillows, so she laid them on the rocks, and let the feathers blow away.

These feathers, wafted by the sea breeze, followed almost the same route as those the Squamish had scattered off Stanley Park in honour of Captain Vancouver nearly ninety years previously.

The loneliness and isolation, and the constant "wash, wash, wash" of the waves on the rocks were too much for the Wellwoods. They left after one year.

Point Atkinson's new lightkeeper, Walter Erwin, and his family, arrived in the fall of 1880 to replace the Wellwoods. Mr. Erwin, one of the original 16 settlers on pre-empted land in West Vancouver, fortunately could not foresee the difficult times ahead in his new job, brought about by the process of change and the challenges of nature.

The family was isolated on the point, with no roads or means of communication with the settlements on Burrard Inlet. One stormy day in 1883, Mrs. Erwin became very ill, and her husband sent a note with two natives passing in a canoe on their way to Moodyville, begging the assistance of a young nurse, Mrs. Susan Patterson. In 1935, her granddaughter, Muriel Crakanthorp, made a record for the Vancouver Archives of her family's recollections of her grandmother's bravery that night, so many years before:

Grandma rushed upstairs and got her things together, and went down to the Indian ranch. The masters of the Etta White and Leonora having refused to put out, the Indians put her into a canoe with blankets, and put out. Two Indians went with her. Some begged her not to go as by this time a regular gale was blowing, but she knew nothing of fear. They made it as far as Skunk Cove, now Caulfeilds, but couldn't reach Point Atkinson as the gale was terrible just there, so they had to tramp from there, the distance being about a mile to the lighthouse through thick forest and rough hills. There was a very small path, but all this took place after dark, and it was very black. One Indian went ahead of her and one behind her and they made the Point Atkinson lighthouse after about four hours from the time they left Moodyville, none the worse for their trip.

Susan Patterson nursed Mrs. Erwin back to health. "The Heroine of Moodyville," a 14-stanza poem by Nora M. Duncan, immortalized her bravery and dedication.

Again, in 1885, a life-threatening situation developed when a forest fire threatened to destroy the lighthouse. With no access other than by sea, Erwin was fortunate to have three men arrive by boat to assist. Using all of the water in the well and the water tower, they managed to extinguish the flames before they reached the buildings.

The duties of the lightkeeper were fairly routine—maintaining a daily log, monitoring and servicing the light, and keeping the buildings clean and tidy. In foggy weather he pumped a hand-horn, made up of twin bellows, when ships' captains signalled with three quick blasts of their horns their need of guidance. In 1889, however, a new innovation, a steam-powered fog horn installed close to the lighthouse, was to add torment to his life. Rather than making his job easier, it virtually ruled his existence. He had to monitor the weather night and day. If visibility closed in to within six kilometres (four miles), he had to shovel coal to raise steam in the "mechanical tyrant," then crawl inside the boiler to clean it out when the weather cleared. In 1896 his logs showed 1450 hours of bad weather. The setting was idyllic, but the life was harsh reality, typical of most pioneers' existence.

Logging and Mining

The 1870s saw a trickle of miners, loggers, fishermen and settlers to Howe Sound's islands and shoreline. Even in nearby Moodyville (now North Vancouver City), Granville and Hastings (townsites on Burrard Inlet) only 146 males (and 14 Chinamen, listed separately) were residents according to the 1874 Victoria Directory. This number did not include loggers or natives. In the New Westminster District (an area that stretched almost as far north as Whistler, west to the Strait of Georgia, south to the United States, and east to Harrison Lake), a survey listed 1356 residents, men and women, but also did not include natives.[4]

The population increased slowly because of the difficulties prospective settlers faced in reaching British Columbia. They had only a few route options, and whichever way they travelled, the trip could last up to five or six months. One choice involved taking a steamer from Britain to the Isthmus of Panama, then a train to the west coast, a steamer to San Francisco and another to Victoria, with delays along the way for making connections. The most time-consuming, but cheapest, was to travel by ship around Cape Horn, then north to Victoria. A third option was cross-country rail travel through the United States to San Francisco, then by ship to Victoria. Wagons, mainly the Red River cart, carried pioneers across Canada on several trails, the most well-known being the Carlton, which reached from Fort Garry in Manitoba to the Yellowhead Pass in the Rockies, a distance of about 1860 kilometres (1160 miles). The rest of the way to the Coast had to be covered on foot or horseback. Little wonder that British Columbia's politicians were adamant that a railway to the coast was one of the conditions for the province joining Confederation.

Still, some settlers and land speculators were interested in the virgin land. Records of New Westminster District, which administered the lands in Howe Sound and the Squamish Valley, show six requests to purchase Howe Sound lots from 1875 to 1877. Four were identified only as being located on Howe Sound, but on October 30, 1875, A.C. Fraser applied for 200 acres (80 hectares) on Gambier Island, and on January 15, 1877, J. H. Privett applied for 40 acres (17 hectares) on Keats Island.

The lure of gold and other minerals enticed prospectors to the area, and they registered several mines. The copper discovered at White Cliff in 1865 led to the formation of Howe Sound Copper Mines Ltd. From then through to the early 1900s, diggings were fairly common around the sound with discoveries of silver and gold as well as copper between the 1870s and 1890s. But none came close to matching Dr. Alex Forbes' discovery at Britannia Mountain around 1890.

Since 1888, Forbes had been medical officer for the natives at Squamish, but he was more keenly interested in prospecting. When a dogfisherman named Granger offered to show him some ore samples and take him to their source for $400, the doctor was skeptical but willing to look. Dr. Forbes told his story to a reporter working for the Vancouver *Province* on May 17, 1931:

He took me almost to the summit of the mountain and showed me the spot he had broken the rock from. There were few places not covered with snow, but we slept that night on the summit. Next morning I began prospecting around the summit, gradually descending towards the valley, without success. About an hour and a half before sunset I saw the famous buck. I shot him in the neck and he kicked around considerably and when I finally got him killed I found he had kicked the moss and rubbage off the rock and there was some good [mineral] showing on the surface. It was getting too dark that night to do anything more, but in the morning I put a shot of dynamite I had with me and found I had got a good showing in place. I then and there paid him the $400 on the *condition that he would not speak to anyone in Howe Sound or Vancouver about it. He agreed and in a few days he bought his boat and went to Alaska.*

So, the first discoverer of copper on Britannia was Mr. Granger, the second was Mr. Buck and the third was Dr. Forbes.

He felt safe leaving the copper claim open, as most miners were looking for gold. He worked at the site every summer and in 1893 took ore samples to the office of the minister of mines in Victoria, to request assistance in developing the claim on Britannia Mountain. He was unsuccessful and lost interest in what would later become the largest copper producing mine in the British Commonwealth.[5]

The infinite forest also attracted men searching for riches. In 1884, Granville's Royal City Planing Mills bought land at Snug Cove on Bowen Island and sent men to begin cutting, the first of several logging operations on the island. The same year, Edward Goudy, a logger working for Moodyville Sawmill, moved his operations from Indian Arm, east of Burrard Inlet, to Howe Sound's western coast. He later told Major Matthews how he cut the timber that reached to the shoreline, cleared a road and built the first buildings on the future site of Gibson's Landing. When George Gibson and his sons first explored the area in 1886, they found stumps and a small log stable, all charred by fire, and skeletons of what appeared to be oxen.[6] This was likely the remains of Edward Goudy's camp, destroyed by a flash fire that burned up the hill from the shore and destroyed the buildings. There's no record of whether Goudy was still there or if he had moved on to a new location.

These early loggers, from 1865 to 1895, used oxen to move the felled trees to the water along skid roads made of narrow logs laid crosswise. The teamster, or bull puncher, saw the animals as slow and stupid beasts, and liberally employed a goadstick and cusswords to move the loads along.

The oxen's hooves were too thin to manage on the rough logs, so they had to be shod. The men would wrap leather straps around the animals' bodies, winch them up above the ground with a hand windlass, then nail on the shoes.

To make the towing easier, a man called a greaser would swab the skids with dogfish oil. Waving his arm back and forth, he spread the oil liberally across the logs and himself. The greaser always smelled so strongly that the rest of the loggers were only too happy to give him his own cabin. Some pioneers earned extra money by catching shark and dogfish, boiling down their livers and selling the oil to the mills for 25 cents a gallon for use on the skids.[7]

About 1895, the time that horses took over from the oxen, some operations built chutes or flumes to carry timber down the hillsides to the water. Flumes were made of sawn lumber. Chutes were made of logs. Some were simply constructed with three logs, one on the bottom and one on each side. Others were much larger and rectangular, with a flat log bottom and two or more logs running lengthwise down each side. They could only be used in wet weather, or with water from a stream running into them, so that the friction of the logs shooting down to the shore would not cause a fire. The logs travelled at such tremendous speed that they would often disappear under the water for some distance before exploding to the surface. Some loggers on the same shores built wide rollways, with the logs laid parallel to the water, and sent their timber tumbling down into the water.

Remnants of an old flume were still evident near Gibsons Creek on Mount Elphinstone in this 1972 photo. *(EPM)*

Logging was a dangerous occupation, and many men were injured, maimed or killed on the job, with no ready medical attention. At Grantham's Landing, a logger named J. McMynn died when he was hit by a log that bounced out of the flume he was using.[8]

By the late 1890s, timber leases dotted Howe Sound's islands and shores and extended north to Whistler. Gambier Island had a shingle mill on the south shore, and across the island to the north, oxen moved logs for a man named Douglas at what was known as Douglas Bay, northwest of Brigade Bay.

In 1895 Edward (Scotty) Wishart and his partner Bill were among the first to live and log at Horseshoe Bay. Their partnership was short-lived as Bill evidently had an aversion to hard work. The workers' bunkhouses and cookhouse took advantage of the view of sea and mountains from what is now the waterfront park.

Tugs and steamboats towed log booms to the mills on Burrard Inlet. The tug *Etta White* moved logs to Moodyville and the *Mermaid* was the towboat for Hastings Mill. Chugging and puffing, she had to carry a large square sail to boost her speed, and towed a scow carrying a load of firewood behind her because she burned so much wood keeping the boilers hot.[9]

Some pioneers had been loggers previously and decided to stay and make their homes on the picturesque land. The new settlers logged their pre-emptions before they could build their homes or plant their gardens. Many cut shingle bolts to earn extra money.

Shingle bolts were always cut from huge old cedars. As the lower portions of the trees were mostly knot free, the men cut the bolts from that part. The tree was cut into 54-inch (137-centimetre) lengths, long enough for three 18-inch (46-centimetre) shingles. These lengths were then split lengthwise into triangular shaped individual shinglebolts easily moved by two men for transport to the shingle mills where they were sawn into shingles. These were flat slabs of cedar, 3/8 inch (9 millimetres) in thickness at one end and 1/8 inch (3 millimetres) at the other. Hand split shakes were used for roofs and walls on early cabins, chicken coops or woodsheds and were split from the edge grain of a cedar block with a maul and froe. The maul was a wooden mallet and the froe was a tool with a handle attached to a piece of flat metal that could be hammered down into the wood to split shakes off.

Sometimes the heavy shingle bolts had to be moved some distance to the water. The settlers usually used horse-drawn wooden sleds called stone boats. These would be positioned at the top of a chute above the shoreline. A scow would be placed at the base of the chute. Then the men pushed the logs down the chute, where they landed on the scow with resounding crashes and bangs. At high tide, a tug pulled the scow off the beach and towed it to a shingle mill.

Early Settlers

In 1885, a man who was to give his name to a town on Howe Sound's coast left Ontario to travel by train across the United States and by steamer from San Francisco, looking for land in British Columbia. George Gibson, a 58-year-old retired Royal Navy lieutenant, and his two sons, Ralph and George, worked for a short time in Granville but soon headed to Nanaimo, probably to find work on the docks there.

While doing odd jobs, he met John Bell, superintendent of the Nanaimo Sawmill. In a 1946 letter to Major Matthews, Mr. Bell remembered him well as a tall, rangy man with a kindly, agreeable disposition and the philosophy that anything he couldn't pay for he could do without.

John Bell recounted his memory of their conversations:

One day he asked me if I knew of any place on the coast where he could take up a piece of land—preferably on the mainland—not isolated— reasonably near some town. "I have a family. I would like to make a home for them some place. I have not many more years ahead of me. I have not money enough to buy a place. What I would like is enough ground to raise vegetables, keep a cow, some chickens and where there is good fishing so I can make enough money selling fish to buy necessities. I'm going to build me a boat, one I can live in and cruise around until I find a place," he announced. "How much will the lumber cost for a double-ender, flat bottom, thirty feet long?" When I told him the price of clear boat lumber thirty feet long, he shook his head. "No, just rough lumber; the cheapest I can buy—knots won't hurt if they are sound."

He and his son built the boat on the beach; I took considerable pleasure selecting the lumber and advising economy in many ways. It was not a craft one could be proud of, but it answered the purpose. His bill for the material was as low as I dared make it without hurting the old man's feelings[$30].

They set out in their flat-bottomed sloop, *The Swamp Angel*, looking for land on Lulu Island in the Fraser River, but a strong wind blew them across the Strait of Georgia into Howe Sound. They stayed overnight on the south shore of Keats Island, then next morning, May 24, 1886, with a strong breeze behind them, decided to explore the mainland shore across Shoal Channel. Here, near the site of the present government

George and Charlotte Gibson, the earliest settlers at Gibson's Landing, c. 1865. These recently discovered photographs were taken before the Gibsons came to British Columbia. *(EPM)*

dock, they landed and liked what they saw. In 1887, George Sr. and his son George pre-empted two lots beside each other. Eighteen-year-old Ralph chose Pasley Island for his pre-emption. The first white settlers had arrived at Gibson's Landing.

Charlotte Gibson, wife and mother, brought the rest of the family with her on the first CPR passenger train to arrive at Port Moody on Burrard Inlet in July 1886. The tug *Etta White* delivered the lumber for the Gibsons' house, the first white man's family home built on west Howe Sound.

This was also an unforgettable year for Granville, which was incorporated as the City of Vancouver on April 6, 1886, with 175 voters living on Burrard Inlet. Two months later, fire obliterated the city, but within a month and a half it was again a going concern.

In 1887, Gibson's son-in-law, George Glassford, and his friend James Fletcher headed west on the CPR and shortly afterwards brought their families to join the Gibsons, loading household possessions and a cow on the scow towed by the reliable *Etta White*. They pre-empted land and shared accommodations with the George Gibsons while building their own small log houses. Money was scarce, so the two men rowed to Vancouver for work, as did many other settlers.

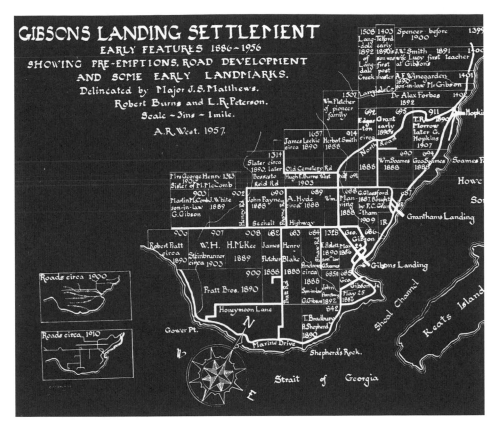

Illustration courtesy Maryann West/EPM

Charlotte Gibson arrived on the first train to arrive at the coast, but the CPR travelled only as far as Port Moody in July 1886. Trains didn't steam into Canadian Pacific's official western terminus at Vancouver until May 23, 1887.

Before the railway had even reached Port Moody, however, the Canadian government, keen to attract settlers, issued a pamphlet entitled "Province of British Columbia: Information for Intending Settlers." Promising that rates for steamer passage plus United States rail travel would be "materially lessened" once the CPR was ready for traffic "early in the spring of 1886," the government encouraged settlers by offering $10 bonus certificates to all immigrants over 16 years of age.

If the influx of settlers to Sea to Sky Country during the next few years was any indication, the CPR did, indeed, open up British Columbia. More and more pre-emptors claimed land on Bowen, Keats, Gambier,

Anvil, and Pasley Islands, at Gibson's Landing and Squamish, and up the Squamish Valley.

Settlers also arrived on the north shore of Burrard Inlet. North of Point Atkinson lighthouse, squatters pre-empted land after the railroad reserves were lifted from North and West Vancouver in 1886. This land had been set aside when the Canadian Pacific considered running its rails there. Nelson Creek received its name from a man named Nelson, a framer at the Hastings Mill, who registered his pre-emption after 1886. An Italian fisherman lived on Eagle Island, which the locals dubbed Italy Island. A Mr. McPherson brought his family to the little bay at White Cliff Point, near Copperhouse Point, north of White Island, which was then called the Bird Rocks. Also near White Cliff, the government settled a group of Newfoundland fishermen in 1888. William Grafton of Bowen Island remembered them in a 1934 interview with Major Matthews.

Did you ever hear about the Newfoundland fishermen's fishing station [near] Whitecliff? The Provincial government located the Newfoundland fishermen on deeded land in the spring of 1888. They were Captain Alcock, Rich Gosse and Andrews; they had three bays, a bay apiece, no men with them, just their families . . . Captain Alcock and Andrews each built a wharf, both in Fisherman's Cove, Alcock to the north, Andrews to the south; Alcock took out the first sealing schooner from Vancouver, the "C.D. Rand."

The Provincial government . . . had to buy them off, for they had put them in at Copperhouse Point (Whytecliff) and there was a dispute about the ownership of the land.

This dispute may have been with the Howe Sound Copper Mines Ltd., the original owner of the land at White Cliff.

Bowen Island

Even though Bowen Island was easily accessible from Vancouver, serious settlement didn't begin there until the 1880s. Joseph Mannion, the well-known owner of the Granville Hotel and alderman in the small town of Vancouver, first bought land on the west shore of Gambier Island in 1884. The creek there still bears his name, although he sold the lot shortly afterwards. He bought another property on the west side of Bowen Island in 1885, sold it, and decided to build a home for his family on a beautiful bay on the east side. He, with his wife, Sabina, and their children, camped for a few years on this lot between Snug Cove and Deep Bay, then made a permanent move to the island in 1888. Joseph was 49 years old and, according to his daughter Margaret, "a tall handsome man of robust frame, well educated, generous to a fault and fond of good music." His land later became known as Terminal Farm. The cove, then called Mannion's Bay, is now Deep Bay.[10]

Joseph Mannion, an early Vancouver alderman. Mannion was an astute businessman, land speculator and well-known Bowen Island resident from 1888 to 1898. *(BIH 145)*

Bill Eaton, Bowen Island's original settler who pre-empted near Killarney Lake in 1874, leased land on the lot next to the Mannions to some Swedish men who wanted to build a brickyard. Deep Bay was a solid bed of blue clay, a valuable resource for bricks needed by the expanding construction industry on Burrard Inlet.

Mannion bought Eaton's land in 1888 and leased or rented a portion to a group of speculators headed by David Oppenheimer from Vancouver. They developed their own brickyard there, on the north side of Killarney Creek, just below Bridal Falls. At first it was run by water power, then by steam. Lee Kee, a Chinese man, won the contract for making their bricks for around $3 per thousand. William Grafton, who settled on Bowen Island around that time, claimed that the bricks from this yard helped build Vancouver's first city hall, Oppenheimer's warehouse at the southeast corner of Columbia and Powell Streets, and the Tremont Hotel on Carrall Street.

Mannion took over the operation of the original brickyard from the Swedes. They had been using horse power, the four-footed kind, so Mannion had a steam plant built and for several years produced popular red bath brick, the type commonly used for construction.[11]

William and Tom Grafton, active young men, arrived with their mother in 1887 and built a cabin on their pre-emption. William, whose accounts of pioneer life recorded by Major Matthews for the Vancouver Archives are an important part of the island's history, started the only ferry service on Howe Sound with his "four ton sloop, no engine, just sails, no name." He recalled,

I ran up and down [Howe Sound] about once a week; had contract with the brick yard [to take bricks to Vancouver], and also made special trips. There were only one or two settlers at Squamish at that time, but there were logging camps up Howe Sound.

I also took the supplies in my sloop for Lee Kee. And the opium. I carried tins of opium too in those days. I first took it as freight; no crime to smoke opium in those days.

His ferry enterprise lasted until the steamboat *Saturna*, 22.5-metres (75-feet) long and screw-propelled, put Grafton out of business.

William Grafton's brother, Tom, later became lightkeeper at Point Atkinson.

From this time until the late 1800s, several families settled on Bowen. Some farmed, some logged and some simply pre-empted or bought from settlers for speculation, either to mine or to hold unoccupied as an investment.

The island was a hunter's dream. The woods abounded with deer and grouse, and the lakes with fish. Some settlers added to their income by selling the wild meat. William Grafton's prize trophy was a 100-kilogram (220 pound) deer. Often they would see the animals swimming to escape the wolves, which became such a danger that the settlers killed them off.

Bowen soon became an attractive picnic spot for visitors from Burrard Inlet. Boat, cabin and tent rentals attracted tourists, and Jacob Dorman later set up a steam-operated merry-go-round and calliope.

The Squamish Valley

The Squamish Valley, a long, hard, 56-kilometre (35-mile) row or sail from Vancouver, did not have the facilities or population for such "frivolous" living. The promising farmlands, the accessibility to water and game, and the undeniably beautiful scenery attracted people to this inaccessible wilderness. Simply to reach their pre-emptions, the earliest pioneers had to exhibit the fortitude and determination that are the hallmark of such adventurers.

The first white settlers were a group of Norwegians who braved the rugged country to settle in the lowlands of the valley in 1885. One of the frequent floods washed away their homes, and they moved away to a new set of challenges.

James Van Braemer and Benjamin Springer received a Crown grant for lot 486 at Squamish on May 4, 1885. Both these Vancouver businessmen were involved with silver mining on Bowen Island, and probably bought the Squamish Valley land as speculators.

The earliest pioneer family to live and stay in the valley were the Alexander Robertsons, who travelled from Manitoba in 1888. They settled near the Mamquam River; their home was the beginning of the town. The next year, their daughter Catherine joined them in February with her husband, Allen Rae. The Raes' son Edgar, born one month later, was the first white baby born in the Squamish Valley.

On October 24, 1889, one of Vancouver's three papers, the *Weekly World*, published an article about H.M. Burwell, a surveyor sent to the Squamish Valley by the provincial government to lay out townships. The constant rain and flooding, and limited social life, led him to suggest tactfully that, "Doubtless, later, Squamish will become a delightful place in which to spend a pleasant holiday." (What red-blooded young man wouldn't miss the social life of the city with only two women around—and both married at that?)

In November 1889, a party of seven men loaded their supplies onto the steamer *Saturna* in Vancouver harbour, and set out for a rugged six weeks on the shore of the Squamish River, with hopes of clearing land for their future homes. The youngest member of the group, 19-year-old Harry Judd, totally inexperienced at outdoor living but going along as cook, recorded their experiences in his diary, which he later mailed to his mother.

With the help of some natives, they paddled and portaged their way up the Squamish River, through rapids and over deadfalls. Judd slept the first night under a bower of cedar boughs and bark on the pre-emption belonging to two of his older companions, Wood and Creelman, north of the Cheakamus River. Working through almost constant rain and later snow, they built a small log cabin, hunted and fished, and assisted other settlers with their tree clearing. Food shortage ultimately reduced them to a limited diet of bread and butter, pork and beans, and tea. As they watched their small supply of food diminish, and the expected native guides did not show up to take them back down the river, they decided to build their own dugout canoe. The natives arrived the day they launched it.

Judd described that trip down the Squamish River on December 20 in his diary: "[The Indians] come along behind to pick us up. We get on a snag before we go half a mile the bow is high and dry out of the water and the stern is near under, the river runs like a mill race. We get off all right and run the next rapids without any accident. In the next we go to take a short cut and run over a log just covered with water. It reminded me of the bumps I used to run over with sleighs."

They fought the wind and waves of a strong gale from the mouth of the Squamish River for the length of Howe Sound, but reached Vancouver safely, in time for Christmas.

The excitement and hardships of a pioneer existence appealed to the young man, and only three months later, in March 1890, he joined his cousin, Bert Chrysler, 21, and friends, Ed Baynes, 19, and H. Drummond, in a grand undertaking. They decided to pre-empt land in the Squamish Valley and set about building a rowboat in False Creek to transport their gear and themselves. They had very little money, so made sails out of bedsheets. Loading up with a shotgun, three axes, a saw, tools, blankets and cooking needs, they set out on March 7 to row the cold and dangerous waters as far as the mouth of the Squamish River. They camped overnight on Bowyer Island and rowed hard the next day, almost reaching their goal, camping below Shannon Falls. They portaged their tiny boat over frozen ground and rowed where possible until reaching their land, 9.5 kilometres (6 miles) up the Squamish Valley, below where the Cheakamus River flows into the Squamish. They spent their first nights under canvas, the snow nearly reaching their knees, but soon cleared an area about three metres square (ten square feet) for a cabin. By May, after weeks of back-breaking work, they had finished a larger log and shake house.

Some excerpts from Ed Baynes' diary illustrate the young men's lifestyle:

May 2—Patterson [another settler] gave us some potatoes and they were a great treat, the first we have had since leaving Vancouver.

*May 4—We take a trip to the lake in the mountains and have a good
time. We got 53 trout and two Blue Grouse which are fine birds being
as large as a good sized hen.*

May 5 to 10—plant seeds—potatoes, lettuce, radish, turnip and beans.

May 15—Chrysler returns from Daisy Lake with 38 trout.

*May 16—visit Vancouver rowing against heavy seas, finally put up
sails around Point Atkinson.*

Probably it was on this trip that one of them accidentally discharged
the shotgun and blew a hole in the bottom of the boat. Only Harry Judd's
quick thinking saved the day. He took off his coat and stuffed it in the
opening until they were able to beach the boat and make a wooden patch.[12]

Harry Judd and Bert Chrysler spent the rest of their lives in the
Squamish Valley, developing prosperous farms. Ed Baynes left after two
years and never returned to his homestead, although Baynes Island bears
his name.

With access to the city only by water, the settlers had to rely on passing tugs and small boats for news and support. During 1890, the steamer
Saturna began once-weekly trips to Squamish, stopping at other islands
en route to deliver supplies and mail. One reporter for another
Vancouver paper, the *Daily World*, decided to visit Squamish, having
heard so much about it, and his article on September 17, 1890, provides
an early picture of the young settlement.

He left on the steamer one morning. It stopped at a brickyard on
Bowen Island, delivered supplies to a logging camp on Gambier Island,
then headed for Squamish, a total run of about six hours from Vancouver.
A small, excited crowd was gathered on the shore at Mashiter's Landing,
hoping for letters and supplies, some meeting friends, and all simply
enjoying a diversion in their isolated lives. William Mashiter's two-and-a-
half storey house became Squamish's badly needed first store. Two years
later, Mashiter opened the first post office in Squamish. He had maintained a love of the Howe Sound lifestyle since he purchased a timber
licence for logging on Keats Island in November 1884.

The reporter's final comments probably reflected the general public
opinion toward those who had no love for the land but saw its availability

The steamship *Burt* at the Squamish wharf, 1894. This gathering may have taken place to celebrate a wedding, but any ship arriving attracted the settlers to collect their mail or greet new arrivals. *(VPL 193)*

only in terms of large financial gain. At the time, 160-hectare (400-acre) lots were selling for $1000. "Here as elsewhere the land grabber has blighted the prospects of settlement by his presence, or rather absence. Of actual settlers in the valley there are only a few, and these are doing good work and will doubtless reap the reward of their labour. Quite a number of those here, however, have no intention of becoming settlers. They are just 'holding down' their claims waiting for a chance to sell. They are worse than the absentee land grabber, if possible."

Anvil Island

Anvil Island, just south of Squamish, is the most isolated and least populated of Howe Sound's larger islands. One man had a dream and brought it to fruition on one corner of the island. His story exemplifies those of many other pioneers who came to British Columbia looking for a new life.

One morning in 1887, Thomas John Keeling went down to breakfast at his home in Staffordshire, England, and announced to his wife and nine children: "I am going to Canada. Who is coming with me?" He departed two weeks later with one son, Shirley, leaving his eldest son, Sam, to take over family and business responsibilities.

The lure of virgin land drew him to Howe Sound on the advice of several prominent men in Vancouver, including Joseph Mannion. His diary from April and May 1887 (now in the Vancouver Archives) describes his search for the ideal homesite. He bought a 6-metre (20-foot) sailboat, and he, his son Shirley, and another young man named Bonson, stocked it with a box of food—flour, bacon, sugar, tea, treacle, etc.—a portmanteau full of clothes, a tent and cooking pots. They set off up the sound, sailing and rowing as far as the Squamish River, sleeping on the ground, visiting islands and mainland shores. Much of the time the wind was against them and they had a great deal of "hard pulling" to make headway.

Plagued by a heavy chest cold, Tom Keeling's actions were restricted: "I had a bad cold when I started which seems to have settled on my chest. I cough and spit a good deal, and if I move about any I am pumped out at once. This may be accounted for in some measure, as I have so many clothes on." After a mustard poultice on his chest, two stiff glasses of whisky and a good night's sleep, he began to recover. His enthusiasm for the beauty of the landscape and the immensity of the trees overcame the disappointment at their poor luck with fishing and hunting.

They first landed on Anvil Island on Monday, April 11, 1887, where they found an old bullock shed left there from an abandoned logging operation. They slept in their tent that night, comfortable on hay from the shed. The next day they discovered some cattle, a small area of cleared land, and a lovely view. He noted: "I like this place very much."

They rowed north to the Squamish River and explored there. He became lost for over four hours in the densely wooded flats. Here Charley, a Squamish native, instructed them on how to catch "Salmon Trout." Returning along the sound's west coast, camping and hunting, they visited Keats and Pasley Islands and had a hard row back to Vancouver. On April 20, after a good meal, he wrote: "I do not wonder at fellows who have been months away from civilization in coming back again having a bash. To have been away 16 days and have had a most interesting trip, tough and uncomfortable at times, but the excitement has carried us well through this.

"Soap and water has not been much used and I have only had my clothes off twice since I was away."

Mr. Keeling immediately began making enquiries in New Westminster and Victoria about available land, but was especially interested in locations on Anvil and Keats Islands.

Joseph Mannion suggested that he and Shirley take a native guide for the second trip, but the cost of $4 per day was too high. They asked Ralph Gibson, the 19-year-old son of George Gibson, to go with them, which he did willingly for $2 per day. Mr. Keeling considered him a strong, active and intelligent lad.

After being held up for several days by storms and winds, on May 5 they arrived on Anvil Island for the second time. He liked it even better this visit, but a potential problem arose: "Found an Indian is living here. I hope there may be no trouble with him. The cattle that are here I expect belong to him . . . We did not see any deer but the Indian who has been living here for the last seven years I hear has 10 or 12 dogs running loose, who have to get their own living and have driven everything from this side of the island." This must have been the case, as the Squamish name for Irby Point, where he wanted to pre-empt, had been Thla-Hoom—"a good hunting place for deer."

The men explored the bays and some of the higher land. Tom Keeling picked out the site for his home on the southern shore at the mouth of a creek, and they blazed several trees to mark boundaries. One they marked "PROSPECT T J KEELING MAY 6, 1887." It was on a line with Centre (now Christie) and Passage Islands.

After again visiting the Squamish River and Charley, they headed south to Keats, then on to Pasley Island where Ralph Gibson had his pre-emption. They stayed overnight on "Whale Island," as it was called because of the earlier whaling operations there, sleeping in an old whalers' hut facing Bowen Island.

The next day they returned to Vancouver. Tom Keeling made plans for pre-empting the southeast corner of Anvil Island, although he would have liked to take it over entirely. His pre-emption remains almost the only occupied land on Anvil Island to this day.

He finished his diary with the following entries:

Tuesday May 17—Back and made up plans of land c/w New Westminster. Saw Mannion, he thinks we should have some difficulty with the Indian on Anvil Island, decided to go to New Westminster tomorrow and see what we can make of it.

Wednesday May 18—Went to New Westminster by stage; saw the Indian agent he advises us by all means to preempt the land on Anvil Island if we fancy it, and he will arrange with the Indian as satisfactorily as he can—Went to land office & took up 320 acres [130 hectares] of land on Anvil Island paying two dollars per. in my name and Shirley's.

Thursday May 19—Making out cost of building house on Anvil Island and writing up this diary.

They cleared the land, built their home and within five years had developed lush vegetable gardens, prolific apple and pear orchards and a herd of healthy cattle. Tom Keeling investigated the quality of the large beds of grey clay on his land, sending samples to England for analysis, and planned for a future brickworks on the island.

In 1888, two other sons, Fred and Tom, joined them from England. Fred pre-empted land on the east shore of Gambier, a short boat ride away, built a sturdy log cabin, and cleared land for a farm.

Their homes were isolated, but Tom Sr. must have kept up social contacts with several Vancouver businessmen. On Sunday, July 22, 1894, the Alhambra Senator Stag Party and Picnic was held on Keeling's land at Ramilles Bay. For 50 cents, participants could enjoy a cruise from Vancouver on the SS *Comox*, have meals and refreshments on board, and visit a remarkably beautiful setting on Anvil Island.

The pamphlet advertising the Party provides a good description of some of the sound's inhabitants and land development at that time:

Rounding the Lighthouse the Queen Charlotte Passage of Howe Sound is entered, Passage Island, belonging to Mr. Keith, being midway between Point Atkinson and Bowen Island. Two miles up on the right are the Bird Rocks, where innumerable ducks and other wild fowl congregate. A mile further is Lagoon Bay, the site of a contemplated saw mill. On the same shore a mile further is Eagle Harbor, the terminus of the Keith Road of North Vancouver; and further still, White Cliff Point, where is a copper mine. There is now a full view of Anvil Island.

On the opposite shore of Bowen Island is Snug Cove and Deep Cove, the residence of Mr. Joseph Mannion. Two miles on same side is the Argyle Silver Mine, on which a good deal of money has been spent. Some persons still think it contains a rich vein. A little further is Hood

Fred Keeling (centre) left England in the late nineteenth century and settled at Halkett Bay at the southeast corner of Gambier Island. His father Thomas (right) pioneered on Anvil Island. The man on the left is Thomas Keeling Jr., Fred's brother. The men often rowed the 8.5 kilometres (5 miles) to and from Thomas Keeling Sr.'s home on Anvil Island. *(CVA OUT P1104 N645)*

Point, where Mr. Keith has a nice place. Crossing the Collingwood Channel is Gambier Island in front—Bowyer Island, belonging to Mr. Lindsay Phillips [a real estate agent who bought it from the original Howse owners], on the right. Passing Halket Point to the left is Ross Castle [Tom Ross, a farmer] on Gambier Island, where the Keeling Brothers and Sisson have a fine ranch of several hundred acres.

The White Rock [Pam Rocks] and Centre Island [Christie Islet] are now before us, which are great breeding places for a variety of ducks— a species of large Gull and Black Curlews, a rather rare bird—in the winter are large flocks of what are commonly called Plovers, about the size of a Snipe, which are very good eating.

There are some Sea Otters in this neighborhood a litter having been bred on Gambier Island last year.

Looking up the Ramilles Passage to the left the Slate Quarry belonging to Mr. Rowland may be seen. This is the place from whence McNabb and Robinson so mysteriously disappeared in 1886.

By this time you will be entering Ramilles Bay, on Anvil Island, the residence of Mr. Keeling, who wishes you a pleasant trip with fine weather, and offers you a hearty welcome to his humble abode.

Four years later, Tom Keeling was experiencing a difficult period in his life. In a May 1898 letter to his son Sam, in England, he complained: "Fred's [his son on Gambier Island] treatment of me has been most brutal the last two years. What with the corns on my feet and every now and then lumbago with a severe pain that seizes me quite suddenly in the stomach and compels me to lie down for half an hour—if I do not do so I am violently sick—my life has been a weary one." Far removed from doctors and a social support group, he appeared to have lost his enthusiasm

The brickworks at Anvil Island, 1910. Thomas Keeling, the first white settler on the island, discovered large clay deposits at Irby point at the south end of the island. In 1897 the Columbia Clay Company started making bricks, and in 1910 the Anvil Island Brick Company took over. Men, shovels and wheelbarrows moved the earth. *(CVA OUT P1100 N641)*

for pioneer living. His three sons, Shirley, Fred and Tom Jr., eventually decided to leave and made their homes in other parts of British Columbia.

Tom Keeling sold a portion of his land north of Irby Point to Columbia Clay Company for use as a brick plant. It operated successfully from 1897, becoming the largest in the province by 1905. Its buildings burned down around 1912, but a second company, Anvil Island Brick Company, produced there from 1910 to 1917.[13]

Thomas Keeling died in 1907, a true Howe Sound pioneer.

By the 1890s, hard-working settlers were clearing land and fueling huge bonfires with undergrowth and stumps, branches and deadfalls. From Anvil Island to Bowen, from Squamish to Keats Island, from Pasley Island to Gambier, the white plumes of smoke rose across Howe Sound like signals spreading the message from camp to camp, "You are not alone."

CHAPTER 6

THE SETTLEMENTS

PREFABRICATED BUILDINGS—KNOCK DOWNS (K.D.)—
SETTLERS' 12 FOOT SQUARE HOUSE, ONE ROOM—$100
TWO STORY HOUSE—$845
SCHOOL HOUSE AND BELL TOWER—$850

—excerpt from the catalogue of British Columbia
Mills, Timber and Trading Company, 1905

Gibson's Landing

During the summers of the 1890s, a tall, clean-shaven man, his kindly face browned by the sun, would often stand at the corner of Hastings and Main (then Westminster Avenue) in the busy little city of Vancouver. His boxes of fresh fruit and vegetables attracted passing housewives, their long skirts brushing the wooden sidewalks. He was particularly well-known for the large, juicy stalks of fresh rhubarb grown on his lush land at Gibson's Landing.

George Gibson, in his sixties and an expert gardener, was selling his produce to earn money for family essentials not available from his garden or the nearby forest. His wife, Charlotte, and the other pioneer women needed a minimum of $10 cash a month to feed their families, a considerable amount of money for them at that time. Their husbands took time away from cutting trees, clearing stumps and digging gardens to explore all possibilities for extra income—working for the government building roads, fishing, logging, and selling shingle bolts. At Gibson's Landing, George Glassford supplied fuel to the wood-burning steamers, and he and his neighbour George Soames took on the back-breaking job of loading gravel from their beaches onto scows that took it to Vancouver for use in concrete construction.

Besides working near their homes, the Gibson's Landing men often rowed or sailed in their small boats across Howe Sound between Keats and Gambier Islands, around Bowen Island, past the dangerous tidal rips at Point Atkinson, and into Burrard Inlet, where they tied up to the

Emma Jane Winegarden (centre), daughter of George and Charlotte Gibson, c. 1910. Farm work was the responsibility of all members of a pioneer family—husband, wife and all the youngsters, such as Emma's two children Gertie and Nelson. *(EPM 1423)*

Vancouver wharfs. There they worked mainly on construction in the growing city and periodically carried essential supplies home to their families. Often they risked their lives as their boats nearly swamped in heavy seas and they had to use the bays on Gambier Island as temporary havens. During one trip, George Glassford and James Fletcher waited out a storm for three days on the island before the waves calmed enough for them to cross Thornborough Channel and return home safely, their wives waiting in an agony of suspense, fearing the worst.

The women lived hard and lonely lives, taking over the men's duties while they were away as well as looking after their homes and children. They cooked on woodstoves and hauled buckets of water from a well or stream. They milked the cows and fed the chickens every day, made butter and bread, and even helped scythe and rake the hay at harvest time, always encumbered by their long dresses. Early pictures show some women with thin, lined faces, all merriment long drained from their eyes.

Charlotte Gibson was an experienced midwife as well as a friendly hostess, but she and other women such as Mary Ann Glassford, Edith Soames and Emma Winegarden had few opportunities for social get-togethers or even sharing afternoon tea. Gibson's Landing had been surveyed in 1889 into 65-hectare (160-acre) plots which separated the families to such an extent that neighbours found it difficult to establish close ties. By 1892, the twenty earliest pre-emptions formed a half-circle with a 2-kilometre (1 1/4-mile) radius from the Gibson home on the waterfront. Men worked at building roads to provide easier contact between residents and to connect the young settlement to Sechelt and Elphinstone. Old skid roads often served as trails or the bases for new roads.

The school road led to the new, one-room, frame school with rows of tall windows along each side and an overhead shelter at one end. The children affectionately called the school "The Barn." A two-door out-house, one section for girls and one for boys, stood near the building. The children had to pump water from a well outside, but when it ran dry they scooped cool drinks from a nearby stream.

Ten boys and thirteen girls were Lucy Smith's first pupils in January 1891. She stood on a platform at the front of the class. Her blackboards were wood painted black. Pairs of students sat in rows at handmade benches with desk tops. The teacher was responsible for lighting the fire in the good-sized wood-burning stove in the centre of the room. Wood and water had to be brought in daily. The fathers took turns cutting the firewood and the mothers voluntarily cleaned the classroom.

In September 1891, William Graham, with a Bachelor of Arts degree, took over instruction and received the same wage as Lucy Smith, $50 a month, a salary that would remain the same for many years in British Columbia. He stayed for five years.

A rural school like the one at Gibson's Landing could open with a minimum of ten students, but needed a minimum of six to remain open. Sometimes the single classroom was not large enough to contain the large number of children from the community. At other times, so few children of school age lived there that parents enrolled children of four years old and younger, just to keep the school open. They would enjoy a ride to school most mornings on their fathers' backs.

On their way to school, the children followed the forest trails, carrying their lunches in metal buckets. The girls skipped along in blouses and skirts, black stockings and ankle-high buttoned shoes, their long hair usually topped with a large ribbon bow. The boys trudged, more unwillingly perhaps, in their long pants, sweaters and boots, caps topping their heads.

The teacher handled discipline with a willow switch, which warmed many students' hands, or assigned long, boring paragraphs for memorization. The strap didn't appear until about 1920. A black book recorded the discipline used and the reason for it. Some entries showed: "two strokes on the back with my pointer for playing across seats; three strokes on the back for persistent turning around in her seat; whipped for persistent disobedience; whipped for persistent talking and laughing." One female teacher at the settlement was unable to manage adequate class control, which encouraged some of the boys to devise many tricks in the classroom, one of which involved shooting wads of paper around the room with springy metal corset stays.

Some pupils were very motivated to learn and the teachers dispensed praise to them in the form of certificates at the end of the school year. Elphinstone Pioneer Museum in Gibsons exhibits a framed certificate presented to Ellen Matilda Gibson in June 1891 for holding first rank in Punctuality and Regularity. Lucy H.B. Smith signed as teacher.

School wasn't all academics. At recess and lunch times the children scrambled through a fort on top of a large stump beside the school building, or played Run-Sheep-Run, Poison-Tag or Hide-and-Go-Seek. Once a month the mothers would bake buns and take them to the school as a treat. The children called this special day "a bun fight," but only they knew whether they used the buns for activities other than eating. Every year they enjoyed their Annual Picnic and held sports day in the spring. The Christmas Concert was the year's highlight, with a large Christmas tree decorating the classroom.

Some of the earliest pioneers at Gibson's Landing stayed on to complete the residency and improvement requirements for a Crown grant, which gave them legal title to their property. Other settlers left by the early 1890s. Gradually, hopeful settlers claimed land along the coastline. The first white baby to start the younger population growth was Grace Glassford, born in 1890. By 1895, the British Columbia Directory, a listing of residents, their occupations, and businesses in British Columbia, showed 51 men as Howe Sound residents, as compared to 33 in 1892. An accurate population size for Gibson's Landing for the period is not available as this number included all of Howe Sound south of Squamish.

As more white people arrived, a small group of Squamish natives returned from the Squamish River reserves to their old reserve on George Glassford's pre-emption directly north of the Gibson's. They fenced it in and built three houses there, using them mainly as a base for fall fishing and hunting and trading some of their meat with the Gibson family for vegetables.

The Gibson men had built a small wharf for their sloop, *Swamp Angel*, and one of the Union Steamship Company's tugs would stop there at irregular intervals and drop off supplies and passengers. Sometimes passengers had to float to the beach on rafts when the tide was too low to permit larger boats to tie up at the dock.

Mail delivery was a problem for Gibson's Landing residents. Their letters, addressed to General Delivery, had to be picked up in Vancouver. George Gibson became the first postmaster for the Howe Sound Post Office on October 1, 1892. The office served all of the Howe Sound communities south of Squamish. Residents could pick up their mail at any time at the small cedar shack behind the Gibson home. Often the flame of a coal oil lantern set on the wharf would reflect on the waves after dark to guide late arrivals. Because other post offices were opening at new settlements around the sound, the government changed the name 15 years later to Gibson's Landing Post Office.

In 1893, the Union Steamship Company's steamer *Comox* began to deliver passengers and mail once a week from Vancouver on its way north up the coast, and sometimes the SS *Capilano* made stops. The company's tugs and passenger ships were a vital element in the development of the Howe Sound communities, carrying building materials, furniture, supplies and people to isolated areas.

Religious services also came to Gibson's Landing by boat as the Thomas Crosby Marine Mission boat used the wharf as its headquarters for several years, serving Britannia and Bowen Island as well as other coastal villages. George Gibson, an active Methodist, held church services and Sunday school in his home until he donated land in 1910 for the community's first church. The small, wooden building had a tiny front porch, a white picket fence, and tall, plain glass windows along each side. Later, stained glass memorial windows replaced them, one in memory of George Gibson.

The settlers also needed a store. On February 21, 1893, Ralph Gibson received the Crown grant to his land on Pasley Island, then sold it two months later and moved to Gibson's Landing. He built the first store that year, but unfortunately went bankrupt before long. The settlers still needed a store, so his energetic father stocked his son's building while he had a new general store constructed at the entrance to the wharf. It opened for business in 1900 and operated successfully, as did most of George Gibson's enterprises, until it burned to the ground in 1910. It was later rebuilt.

In a 1902 Public Works report, foreman R.F. Bonson reported that a 30- by 70-foot [9- by 22-metre] wharf had been constructed near the Gibson home, with a shingled wooden storehouse and a slip, all supported by three rows of driven piles. This made the deliveries by tug and steamship much easier and encouraged the Steamship Company to stop there more often.

A group of Finnish settlers arrived at Gibson's Landing in 1905 from their previous homes, most on Malcolm Island off northern Vancouver Island. Others later immigrated from Finland. They formed a close-knit, hard-working group that contributed to the area's social and economic development. Their presence on the plateau above the coast, Gibson Heights, encouraged the establishment of a store and post office there. The Ruises, Hintsas and Lantas, the Wilanders, Wilkmans and Wirens purchased land, developed farms and built the first community hall in the district. Wiljo Wiren was a child at the time, but in his nineties he remembered weekly musical gatherings with Finnish dances that also attracted some English-speaking settlers.

A year after the Finnish settlers' arrival, the terror of fire descended upon the plateau above Gibson's Landing. Started as a brush burn-off, it spread out of control from East Roberts Creek towards the sound, incinerating all trees and undergrowth in its path. Some homesteaders fought to keep their homes wetted down with barrels of water on the roofs, while others fled the flames. Fortunately only one life was lost and very few homes burned, but the forest was a desolation of burned snags pointing skyward above the bare and blackened ground for about an eight-kilometre (five-mile) stretch.

Squamish

Despite the pioneers' apparent isolation, similar growth was taking place not too far away across Howe Sound's waters. The 1892 British Columbia Directory was enthusiastic in its description of the Squamish Valley:

A beautiful valley situated at the head of Howe Sound about 35 miles distant from Vancouver city, containing an area of about two miles in width, and twenty in length. It is well adapted for all kinds of agricultural purposes. Hop growing is likely to become one of the principal industries of the place, as they seem to do remarkably well here. Cattle do well all winter. There is a large tract of timber on the north east end. This valley is drained by three rivers, Squamish, Mamcum [Mamquam], Cheacamus [Cheakamus], all of which abound with salmon and trout.

When the road now being built is completed, there will be a very enjoyable drive, also excellent hunting. Quite a lot of visitors come up in the summer and return very much pleased, and congratulate the inhabitants on having one of the best valleys in British Columbia. An immense seam of hard coal has been found in the near vicinity. The hotel kept by Mr. Mashiter affords good accommodation for visitors. There is steamer communication once a week to the head of the Sound. Game is in abundance ranging from a grouse to a grizzly. The clearing up of land is steadily increasing and the area of cultivatable lands extended. Plums, apples, pears, currants, gooseberries and all kinds of small fruits do remarkably well. The speculators and Indians hold quite a lot of good land.

The Directory listed 29 men's names as Squamish residents. Almost all were farmers except William Mashiter who was a storekeeper and postmaster, and Ebenezer Madill, a farmer and butcher. The next year the post office also provided telegraph and express services to the population of about 40 people.

On September 6, 1892, the Vancouver *News Advertiser* published a notice of application signed by three McIntosh brothers and E.W. Wright to have the area incorporated as a municipality. The Vancouver *Daily World* announced on October 12 that same year that the settlement had been incorporated and "would no doubt derive the benefits which flow from [this] measure placing the control of its affairs in the hands of its residents."

By 1894, Squamish boasted a schoolhouse that doubled as a public hall (the teacher was E.G. Magee). The September 26 *Daily World* advertised twice-weekly steamer connections to Vancouver, encouraging travellers to and from the city. Community affairs were expanding.

Since 1892, the Horticultural Society and Fruit Growers' Association of British Columbia had provided the opportunity for the farmers on Howe Sound to keep in touch with what was happening in other parts of the province. E.B. Madill from Squamish and George Gibson of Gibson's Landing were two of the directors. The Squamish Valley was fruitful, and yearly floods promised one advantage—they added fresh soil to the bottom lands. Fruit, hay and root crops were popular, but the *Daily World* of October 12, 1892, reported that several of the farmers, including Mr. Madill, began to include hops as a major crop since the soil and climate seemed perfectly suited to its growth. By 1895 he had about two hectares (five acres) devoted to hops. They were to attract strong commercial interest in the valley.

The January 1893 annual report of the Horticultural Society included the details of a speech by William Shannon, the president of the Squamish Valley Hop Raising Company, formed the previous year. He reported that the cost to them of clearing and stumping the land was about $100 per acre (.4 hectare), and at this time they had planted about three acres (a little more than one hectare). Their hop farm was on the west side of the Squamish River, not far north of the confluence with the Mamquam River, land they had held since 1889 as speculators. Optimistically he stated that they hoped to harvest 1500 to 1600 pounds (700 kilograms) to the acre, and in the next year to have cleared several hundred acres. Their $10,000 capital investment paid off, as the company was in business until the First World War caused a drastic drop in hop prices.

William Shannon and his partner, Charles McLachlan, were experienced entrepreneurs. Shannon had started a business in 1889 at Darrell Bay, just south of Squamish at the foot of Fairy Falls (now Shannon Falls), producing and selling bricks formed from the large clay deposits around the stream leading to the bay. The two men recognized a good potential for hop growing, as did many of the local farmers—Allen Rae, Tom Reid and G. Magee among them—and moved their business interest to the development of that product. The *Daily World* reported on September 26, 1894, that both Ebenezer Madill and the Squamish Valley Hop Company employed natives to pick the quality crops on their ranches. The hops, tied in 46-kilogram (100-pound) bales, eventually went to England.

In 1893, *Williams British Columbia Directory* shows the Vancouver Hop Company (later the Pioneer Hop Ranch) hired Frank Potter as foreman to oversee the clearing of 11 hectares (28 acres) in Brackendale. As their hop fields ripened, they also hired Squamish natives who travelled on horseback and brought their wives and children and dogs with them. On Sundays they entertained the settlers with exuberant horse races up and down the valley, their yapping dogs bringing up the rear.

New homes were appearing throughout the settlement, often built by groups of helpful neighbours at house-raising bees. Harry Judd, who by 1894 was a serious farmer, needed a home for his future family. In December, friends helped him to raise his new 5.5- by 7.2-metre (18- by 24-foot), storey-and-a-half log house. It was located so close to the forest that he could stand at his back door and shoot his winter's meat supply.

Judd would not be able to attend many more bachelor entertainments, as he was soon to marry Barbara Annie Edwards. She had come to Squamish that year as a helper for Mrs. Alice Rose, whose husband, Charlie, worked at the Vancouver Hop Company. Harry Judd's father, Thomas, his mother and the rest of his family came from London, Ontario, the next year, and both men farmed.

Barbara and Harry were to have two sons and eight daughters, and with the Raes' eight sons and two daughters, the two families amply swelled the new community's population.

Squamish was receiving more and more visitors after the Union

Steamship Company initiated a weekly service to the Squamish River (and three-day-a-week service to all points on Howe Sound) on July 12, 1891. The first day-excursion to the Squamish Valley, August 1, 1891, was a group from the Women's Hospital Society of Vancouver to raise money for a new hospital.[1]

As in Gibson's Landing, social contact was limited by lack of roads. The isolated farms in the Squamish Valley and Brackendale were some distance from the townsite. Some people were also looking for the means of travelling to and from the interior along the Pemberton Trail. Settlers heading north to Alta Lake, Pemberton and the Cariboo counted on the pack trains from Squamish to carry household articles and supplies, although the packers charged as much as three cents a pound and were consistently hindered by winter snow.

The provincial government again had foreman R.F. Bonson busy with his crew. By 1895 they had built, and later repaired, a bridge across the Squamish River and opened a new road up the Cheakamus River. The Public Works report for that year noted the "opening of 120 chains of a road from the north end of the Cheakimus [Cheakamus] bridge and extending up the Cheakimus Valley on the west side of the river to give an outlet to Messrs Hayden and Anderson and others (voluntary labour of Hayden and Anderson)." Obviously farms were extending farther up the valley.[2]

A 20.5-kilometre (12 3/4-mile) sled trail, 5 metres (16 feet) wide, opened the upper Squamish Valley at a cost of $1445, and in the same year, 1895, Bonson's crew constructed the first steamer wharf at the Howe Sound shoreline, 7.3 by 11 metres (24 by 36 feet) on 14 piles. The cost was $180.

The Pemberton Trail was becoming increasingly more important as a means of access to, and exit from, the interior for prospectors, packers taking supplies to Pemberton, and families heading that way to settle. The government hired surveyors in 1895 to carry out a Location Survey and had bridges repaired along the route. Improvements continued after the turn of the century. They kept the trail open for 96.5 kilometres (60 miles). The old Moodyville Trail, part of the Pemberton Trail that ran from Squamish to Seymour Creek in North Vancouver, must still have been in use as, in 1902, Mr. Bonson reported that he and his men cleared, brushed and logged 16,093 metres (52,800 feet) of it to a width of 3.1 metres (10 feet).

James George Rougier's pack train carrying supplies along the Pemberton Trail, 1911. A resident of Vancouver, Rougier pre-empted land near Mount Currie in the 1890s, then bought property on Green Lake. *(AM)*

Harry Judd used the Squamish to Brackendale section of the roads to operate the first stage. He met steamer passengers at the wharf with his wagon, pulled by two horses, and took them on a rather bumpy ride to their destinations in the valley. For $2.50 he also provided a day-long outing for visitors. He probably also delivered mail to the Brackendale post office, which opened in 1906 and was named after the first post-master, Thomas H. Bracken, and the fields of bracken which grew close by. In 1911, Judd upgraded to a much noisier, motorized passenger vehicle, the first in the valley to be used as a stage. It was able to carry 15 people.

Some of the steamer passengers were heading farther north than Brackendale, as the word was spreading about the breathtaking scenery and the excellent fishing and hunting. Alice Lake, just east of Brackendale and named after a Squamish settler, Alice Rose, was a favourite picnic and hiking destination. A campsite at Daisy Lake served

The J.T. Lake Hardware Store, Squamish, 1910. In front of the store are Henry Judd's motorized stages—the first in the area—waiting to take passengers to Brackendale. *(SPL 8.27)*

most of the travellers, but a couple of intrepid men recognized the potential for increased use of the Pemberton Trail and, in the early 1900s, built log cabins for stopping houses where passers-by could spend the night and purchase a meal. One of these establishments—Cotton's, on Green Lake—had a good-sized log house on land that Cotton had purchased from another adventurer, "Cheque-Book" McDonald. This venture was not successful and he eventually left the cabin deserted.[3] Further south though, beside what is now Alpha Lake at Whistler (then known as Millar's Lake), John Millar's small wooden Halfway House was a popular spot for travellers. They could get a good meal for 50 cents, and a soft bed, sometimes in the haymow, also for 50 cents.

"Mahogany John" Millar told many stories, both about his past and his habits, and became the topic of many pioneers' conversations. One Pemberton settler described Millar's unique culinary style for the book *Pemberton: The History of a Settlement*: "He threw slices of bacon from table to frying pan, never missing. When everything was ready he would remove the stub of a cigarette from his lips and utter the words well known to every Pemberton pioneer, 'Now, gentlemen, please put your feet under the mahogany'."

A short man with a flattened nose and a booming voice, John liked to entertain visitors with his own introduction:

I am Miller [sic] of Chekacamus Flats
I'm wild and woolly and from the west.
I'm full of burrs, I'm full of fleas,
I live on the grass and the prickly pears.
I never was curried below the knees.
And I play with the grizzly bears.

During the winter months, he was completely isolated from the outside world and spent his time trapping and hunting marten, lynx, wild cat and other animals in the snow.[4] He told the developers of Whistler's first lodge about Alta Lake.

In 1908, one group of adventurers from Vancouver took the steamer to Squamish, rented horses from Galbraith, who was owner of the Squamish Hotel, and followed the Pemberton Trail north. Their horses took them along the Cheakamus River, over rockslides, through Bear Canyon, into deep valleys, past Desolation Pool and Stony Creek (now Rubble Creek) and on to Daisy Lake, which they described as nothing more than a shallow slough, circular in shape, like the crater of a long-extinct volcano. When they reached Millar's place, after suitable refreshment and rest, they assembled their collapsible canoe and used it to pull in dozens of trout from Millar's lake. They were astounded that on four separate occasions, three fish were hooked at one cast, but catching two fish at a time was common. Millar traded

John Millar, the man who introduced Alex and Myrtle Philip to Alta Lake, c. 1918. Millar lived in a small cabin near what is now Whistler's Function Junction. *(WMA P86.1324)*

James George Rougier's temporary General Store on Green Lake, just north of Alta Lake beside the Pemberton Trail, 1911. Rougier's home and permanent store building, visible in the background, are nearing completion. *(WMA)*

bread for the fish, as he could use them in the winter to bait his animal traps. The travellers later portaged about 1.5 kilometres (1 mile) north to Summit Lake (now Alta Lake) where "nothing was left to be desired" with the scenic beauty, the weather and the fishing. Frank Burnett described their experiences in the December 1908 issue of *Westward Ho!* magazine.

On their trip back to Vancouver, the men would have passed a set of small islands to their right, like stepping stones leading to Anvil Island. These are the most easterly in a collection of more than 13 individual islets and rocks, spread over half a kilometre, called the White Rocks (now Pam Rocks). A little more than a kilometre to the north is Centre or Gull Island (now Christie Islet). They were, and are, an important breeding location for seabirds. According to August Jack Khahtsahlano, the natives called them Kwa-Layt-Kum—"Where the sea gulls Hatch."

Bowen Island

Midway between Squamish and Vancouver, Bowen Island was attracting visitors less inclined to the adventurous trips to the Squamish Valley and beyond. Joseph Mannion and his wife, Sabina, offered hospitality that attracted visitors to their home at picturesque Mannion's Bay (later Deep Bay) on Bowen's eastern shore. The Mannions' house was a large, stately building with outside walls of finished lumber, likely from a Vancouver mill. A verandah with railings enclosed the front entrance, and three brick chimneys dotted the peaked roof.

Not all early homes were as expensively constructed as the Mannions'. Many settlers could afford only to pre-empt and build their own rough cabins. Edward and Mary Galbraith's small cabin at Galbraith Bay on the island's northwest side was made of squared-off logs the size of mature tree trunks, with the cracks well chinked against the weather, and a cedar shake roof. Bessie Galbraith McIntosh wrote, in a 1970 letter to the Bowen Island Archives, that when the family moved in in 1899, it had no windows and only an open doorway. Later, a door flanked by two windows was added. Mr. Galbraith had brought them with his family—along with chickens, berry bushes and furniture—on a fishing boat rowed from Vancouver. Eventually a small front porch provided a cozy gathering place where the family could sit and enjoy the view over their property, which they proudly called "Westcliff."

While log homes were constructed by hand from available timber, another common type of house had vertical siding of cedar splitboards. These boards were about 1.5 metres (5 feet) long. The higher strips overlapped the lower halfway down the walls, producing a ruffled effect. The same long shakes covered the roof, and the resulting shape was very different from the one created by the shorter cedar shingles that were used more generally. Usually these homes were small and rectangular, with one or two windows. Outside most houses, a pile of firewood with a sawhorse and chopping block stood ready.

About 1892, a group of four men sailed from Vancouver for a surprise visit to the Mannions' home. A.P. Horne recalled their welcome in a later interview with Major J.S. Matthews: "He asked us where we were going to sleep, and we said we had a tent and were going to sleep on the beach. But he said that we were to take the barn. So we slept in the barn, and about daylight a horse poked his nose in the door, and gave a mighty snort, which woke up all, and we turned over and went to sleep again,

Bessie Galbraith's home, overlooking Galbraith Bay on Bowen Island, c. 1899. It was built by her father, E.D. Galbraith, from hand-hewn logs. *(BIH 91)*

and presently Joe appeared in the door, and said we were to come in for breakfast. He said he was so glad to see 'a face' that he could talk to; it was rather lonely, and he was glad to have a visitor. Fine old kindly gentleman, Joseph Mannion."

Because Bowen Island was so much closer to Vancouver than the rest of Howe Sound's settlements, the island lifestyle reflected the more frequent contacts with the city of Vancouver, which made the task of earning extra money for basic supplies much easier. Those settlers with small farms could row to the city in half the time it took the Gibson's Landing men. They traded butter, eggs, vegetables and fruit at Woodward's store for staples and chicken feed.[5] The men also sold otter and mink pelts in Vancouver.

William Grafton told Major Matthews of prolific schools of herring, 30- to 40-pound (13- to 18-kilogram) salmon, cod and shark off the shores of the island. He and his brother would set their lines overnight, then first thing in the morning they would load their catch into their boat and sail or row to Vancouver, depending on the weather. They sold their salmon to the Hotel Vancouver or a butcher, and later to a company called Winch and Bower, for four to eight cents a pound. The Chinese men who worked at the brickyard beside the Mannions' home would cut off the sharks' fins for soup, a gourmet treat. Each shark liver was large enough to fill a ten-gallon keg. The Grafton brothers rendered them down for the oil. Venison and grouse hunted on the island, and trout caught in the lakes were also popular in the city.

Bowen's farms produced well, providing not only fruit and vegetables, but also hops, which grew as well as they did in Squamish. The central valley area was the best for gardens. Farmers tilled their land with hand-guided plows pulled by horses. Split-rail fences, sometimes topped by barbed wire, surrounded the fields.

Logging continued to provide extra income for some settlers. Skid roads for the logs crisscrossed the island and became bases for permanent

A horse logging operation near Grafton Bay, Bowen Island, 1911. The earliest loggers used oxen, then horses to move timber to the water. *(BIH 42)*

roads. The Public Works report for the year ending December 31, 1897, noted: "Forest cleared one mile, 12 feet wide, corduroyed 100 yards [referring to logs laid crosswise to form a road], 10 feet wide, took out four large cedars, five feet in diameter, and repaired road generally. Cost about $452.44."

About that time the homesteaders had the use of a floating wharf and later a road was constructed from the wharf to the schoolhouse. The school, a frame building almost identical to the one at Gibson's Landing, stood on one corner of the Mannion lot in 1893, located so that children from around the island could follow existing wagon roads or trails through the woods to get to their little red schoolhouse. Some had to walk 3 to 4 kilometres (2 or 3 miles) each way, rain or shine. William Acheson taught 16 pupils the first year. They used chalk and slates, were warmed by a woodstove, and felt the majestic gaze of Queen Victoria watching from above the blackboard, the crossed Union Jack and Canadian Red Ensign flags forming a base for her picture. Two tin cups and a metal pail filled with fresh water were available for thirsty mouths. The pupils learned reading, writing, penmanship, spelling, hygiene, history, geography, water-colour painting, drawing, nature study and music. Parents were active in the school's administration and upkeep, although the school trustees of 1896 voted to pay one of the scholars a dollar a month to keep the schoolhouse clean and light the fire.

By 1898, the Mannion children were in their teens and needed a high school education. The family moved to Vancouver for the schooling, leaving behind many memories and good works. Not very long after the Mannions resettled, their two sons, Clarence and Gerald, drowned in a boating accident while they were rowing back to Bowen Island. Their bodies were never found.

The first school on Bowen Island, 1893. Ten pupils were enrolled and William Acheson was the first teacher. The school was built on a corner of Joseph Mannion's property. Church services were also held there. *(BIH 85)*

The school building hosted church gatherings as well. Reverend Elihu Manuel, a Methodist missionary in charge of the Howe Sound mission who also conducted services at Gibson's Landing, rowed over to Bowen occasionally, and the Methodist mission boat stopped once in a while.[6] But Reverend Ebenezer Robson, a veteran Methodist missionary from the gold camps to Moody's Mill, at age 68 committed himself to conducting regular services on the island. Arriving early Sunday mornings by steamer at Snug Cove, he enjoyed presenting his sermons, developing a Sunday School, and talking with the island residents and visitors.

A post office opened in 1894 in the Beckers' home at Surrey Cove (now Miller's Landing), with Dewitt Becker, an early pioneer, and later his wife Lucia as postmaster. The office took up a small area in one room of their home, which stood high on a rocky bluff above the ocean. A Union steamship, the *Burt*, delivered mail once a week on its way to other points around the sound. The postmaster had a long trek in every type of weather down a steep path leading to the beach, then a hard row out to pick up the mailbag, thrown from the steamer's deck. Mr. or Mrs. Becker then had to face the climb back up the rocky path, carrying the mailbag, clothing catching on branches and brambles. Even then, "The mail must go through!"[7]

William Davies, a pioneer and market gardener at Snug Cove since 1887, later opened the island's first store there, which he ran until the Union Steamship Company opened a large new one in 1925.[8] Davies also ran the post office for 19 years.

The residents lived quiet lives, caring for their farms and gardens, keeping poultry and cows, hunting and fishing, but they were not as isolated as those pioneers on Howe Sound's other shores and they planned weekly social get-togethers, often holding sing-songs around the Smith family's organ. Bessie Galbraith McIntosh, who lived on the island during her early teen years, remembered: "We children loved the whole experience, even bringing of water from the spring in small pails, gathering bark and chips [for firewood], or roaming the beaches and rocks, fishing for shiners, rock cod or perch (which we called sea bass)."

Picnickers and campers from the city had been enjoying weekend trips to the island for some time. Picnickers at that time wore their Sunday best. A photo from the Bowen Island archives shows ladies in toe-length skirts, long-sleeved blouses and wide-brimmed hats; men in dark suits, white shirts, ties and hats. Even small boys wore suit jackets, knee-length knickers, black stockings and caps. Set in a grove of trees near

Jacob Dorman's steam-powered merry-go-round, c. 1900. It was very popular at the Bowen Island picnic area near Snug Cove, but he never ran it on a Sunday. *(BIH 42)*

Snug Cove, and covered with a pointed canvas roof, Jacob Dorman's merry-go-round and calliope played its repertoire of three tunes, providing lighthearted entertainment for five cents a ride. As popular as it was, however, Dorman would not run it on a Sunday.

Several financially well-to-do families from Vancouver bought large pieces of land for their personal estates—George Cowan, a lawyer, at Point Cowan at the southeast corner of the island in 1899; J.C. Keith, manager of the Bank of British Columbia, from William Simpson at Hood Point, the northeast promontory, before 1900; and James Malkin at King Edward Bay, on the island's west side, in 1910.

While these men's plans were to protect and enjoy the serenity of large tracts of the island, the dynamite plant established at Tunstall Bay, near the southwest corner of Bowen, seemed an environmental antithesis. George Tunstall was the sales manager when Western Explosives, a Montreal company, began production there in 1909, employing about 80 men. The white men and their families lived in cottages and bunkhouses, but the Asian workers had to live separately. The settlement was known as a "pretty wild old place" according to William Grafton, probably

A four-masted sailing ship loading explosives at the wharf on Bowen Island, c. 1915. Western Explosives built a dynamite plant at Tunstall Bay on the south shore of Bowen, and during its operation several workers were killed by explosions. Later it was bought by Canadian Explosives and moved to a new location. *(BIH 41)*

because of the parties that went on there. The factory buildings abutted the shoreline, where a long wharf provided moorage for four-masted sailing ships and steamers picking up shipments of powder.

The plant had barely begun to reach its capacity of 400 cases of dynamite and 400 kegs of black powder a day, when the first explosion killed six men. The following year, another employee died from burns after he lit his pipe. The match flame ignited his clothing, impregnated with explosive powder. Stringent safety regulations came into effect after a massive packing house explosion in 1910 that killed five employees. People in Nanaimo, across the Strait of Georgia, heard and felt the blast. As a result, the owners had to provide books of instruction in Chinese as well as English, although some of the Asian labourers couldn't read. Canadian Explosives bought the company in 1911 and later moved the plant to James Island, north of Victoria off the coast of Vancouver Island. Explosives Creek still flows into the Strait of Georgia from Bowen Island.

A different type of commercial venture was the Howe Sound Hotel, built just south of Hood Point in about 1895. It was the first hotel on the island. Visitors to the hotel, very often well-to-do yacht owners from Vancouver, could anchor in what is now Cates Bay. They rowed to the beach, mounting the steps from the wharf and boathouse to the two-storey, frame hotel. Another photo in the Bowen archives shows that the dark paint of the outside walls was attractively highlighted by white trim on the railings of the upper balcony and lower verandah and around the tall windows facing the mountains of the eastern Howe Sound shore. Proprietor Arthur Newland, who also owned the Central Hotel in Vancouver, rented the land from J.C. Keith.

The hotel was a weekend mecca for boat owners and their friends, who were often wealthy foreigners from as far away as Australia, Hong Kong and England. Vancouver Yacht Club members met there and, according to comments in the hotel register, had rather enthusiastic parties. The resort was also a good stopping-off place for loggers rowing from weekend outings in Vancouver, heading back to their camps on Howe Sound. A cold drink and a good meal strengthened them for the last lap.

Most settlers were able to eke out a living with their fishing, farming and logging, and a few started small businesses around the sound. Early in the 1900s, however, more serious business enterprises were to produce a lasting impact on the entire area.

CHAPTER 7

THE SERIOUS BUSINESS

*Plans have been made for the erection of huge elevators for the trans-
shipment of grain to the steamers which will bear it to Europe. And
where there are elevators one will also find flour mills and this will be
the case for Newport [Squamish] for, in addition to the elevators,
mills have also been planned for the running of which there seems to
be an abundant supply of power in sight. This city will also be the
first market for the farm produce of the great fertile valley which
will be opened up by the PGE Railway. [There] will be great railway
development bringing with it shops, mills, factories, docks and ocean
trade. Thousands of families will find remunerative employment.*

—Vancouver *News-Advertiser*, October 20, 1912

Britannia Mine

A lone prospector searched for his bonanza high in the mountains above
Howe Sound's eastern shore. Oliver Furry, a poor and illiterate trapper
from McNab Creek, halfway between Gibson's Landing and Squamish,
scrabbled across rockslides, slid into gullies and pushed through dense
underbrush, chipping at any rock that showed a gleam of ore.
Encouraged by an enthusiastic Vancouver businessman, W.A. Clark, who
offered financial assistance for licensing, recording fees and a grubstake
in exchange for a share in the profits, Furry took out prospecting licences
in the late 1890s and staked five claims in the vicinity of Britannia
Mountain where Dr. Alex Forbes had made his copper discovery ten years
earlier.

When Oliver Furry returned to the city with over 90 kilograms (200
pounds) of rock samples, he enthusiastically reported to his backers that
he had found a mountain of ore. The excitement of a great discovery ran
high, one assayer reporting that the rocks showed 75 percent copper. The
financial backer procrastinated because of personal commitments, but
Furry did not, taking on Thomas Turner and Joseph Boscowitz and his
two sons as partners. Furry staked three more claims in 1898. Other

prospectors, hearing about the find, followed his lead and registered several claims nearby.

In 1900, the Britannia Copper Syndicate was formed by the first group of businessmen to realize the potential and organize. The Boscowitz family, F.M. Leonard and H.T. Cepperly were among the group that approved a memorandum of association for the syndicate. Oliver Furry still retained his 50 percent interest. This was the first opportunity for large business investment on Howe Sound. The public could buy shares in the syndicate for $800 to $1000 each. The syndicate purchased the waterfrontage at the foot of the mountain and bought Fairy Falls (now Shannon Falls) for generation of electrical power. Financial problems stood in the way of its carrying out further plans, and Furry was told that he would have to reduce his interest to 20 percent to help out. In 1901, an American, George Robinson, obtained a controlling interest and in 1903 he began development of what was to become the world-famous Britannia Mine.

For Oliver Furry, the big world of business was too much. Disputes arose about the legality of his contract with the Boscowitz family and his own agreement to accept a 20 percent rather than 50 percent interest. Evidently the worry and confusion drove him insane and he died in 1905 in the asylum in New Westminster. The next year the courts upheld the legality of his claim and agreed that he had not signed the reduction agreement. His brother Ira benefitted. (Oliver Furry died before he could reap the benefits of his discovery, but his name remains in the Howe Sound area. Residents called one of the rivers that fed water to Britannia, South Valley. It later was formally renamed Furry Creek. In the 1990s, a large golf course and housing development opened there.)

Before long, 180 tonnes (200 tons) of rock per day were coming out of the mountains, and land was cleared for a townsite at the beach. The addition of a large dock, office building, hotel, store, a concentrator and crushing plant, and some homes turned the beach into a noisy beehive of activity. Camps established higher up the mountain were isolated home bases to several families who had to travel on aerial tramways from the shore to reach their small cabins. The Jane, or 1050 (Ten-Fifty), Camp was the highest at 1050 feet (320 metres), the distance measured from the highest point of the developed mining area, which was considered zero feet.

In 1908, the Britannia Mining and Smelter Company was formed when the Syndicate purchased the Crofton smelter on Vancouver Island.

A loading depot on Howe Sound, 1912. The ore mined at Britannia was crushed and ground in the mill (or concentrator), then the valuable minerals were carried by conveyor to the loading area and shipped to a smelter on Vancouver Island. *(PM)*

Now the company owned the mine and its own smelter.

As the company hired more men, the need for family and bachelor housing grew, and rows of houses lined the Beach townsite. Harriet Backus, the wife of a mineral assayer, enthusiastically wrote of her life there from 1910 to 1912 in her book *Tomboy Bride*. She described her arrival with her husband, George:

A Japanese deck hand cast off the mooring lines, and the Britannia toot-ed farewell and headed up the Sound. We rounded a corner of the large mill, and after a short walk George unlocked the gate of a picket fence.

"Well, sweetheart, here we are!"

"Good heavens, George!" I stared at a white, six-room palace with living room, dining room, bedroom, kitchen, pantry, bathroom, and storeroom, with doors between rooms and electricity throughout. There were simple if not elegant furnishings.

"Wonderful, wonderful!" And to think only five dollars a month.

Once the couple and their small daughter had settled in, Harriet dis-covered even more attractive features:

There was no need to order ahead and store food as all we needed was just across the road where prices were a housewife's dream. Beef was twenty-five cents a pound, including T-bone steaks . . .

Coal cost six dollars a ton; electricity cost nothing. Water was not only free but abundant and piped to our houses. Beyond bare necessities we had no place to spend money.

The only road, muddy and deeply rutted, led from the dock to the company store. Here the residents could purchase groceries, clothing and other basic needs. The post office, with numerous cubbyholes for mail, had occupied a corner of the store since 1907.

Three boarding houses provided bachelor living space—one for Chinese, one for Japanese, and one for white labourers. A dance hall, an office building and a one-room schoolhouse for the four school-age children were part of the community. Only the quay and large ore bunkers at the shore marred the beauty of the surroundings.

Although the company built a new six-storey mill that could process 1800 tonnes (2000 tons) of ore per day, and production increased, copper prices dropped, causing financial concerns. These were alleviated

Johan Malm, a mine employee, and his family in their cabin at Britannia Mine's Jane Camp, also called 1050 Camp (it was 1050 feet below the highest mine level), c. 1908. Elizabeth Malm reads tea leaves while her husband and their two children, Ernst and Carl, watch. *(PM)*

when First World War armament needs increased copper production to the extent that the mine reached its capacity and set a record for output.

The optimistic spirit generated by the high copper prices was shattered by a devastating blow. On March 21, 1915, the mountain face collapsed above the highest workers' settlement, the 1050 or Jane Camp. An avalanche of mud, snow and rocks roared down the cliff face, engulfing the miners and their families as they slept. It killed nearly 60 people and injured 22 others. The stunned survivors and men from the Beach townsite dug through the rubble, responding to muffled cries from the darkness. Vancouver residents did not hear the news until the next morning, when an exhausted employee rowed to Horseshoe Bay to send out an appeal for medical help. The recovered bodies, in rough wooden boxes, made their last trip to Vancouver on the SS *Ballena*, while grieving residents watched and the ship's flag flew at half-mast. Some bodies still lie on the mountain, buried under tons of debris.

The company, in the interest of safety, constructed a new townsite farther down the mountain at the 2200-foot (670-metre) level, which was closer to the mine workings than the Beach townsite at the 5700-foot (1730-metre) or sea level. The new site became known as the Townsite

On March 21, 1915, an avalanche of mud, snow and rocks engulfed Britannia Mine's highest townsite, the 1050 or Jane Camp, killing nearly sixty people in their beds. *(VPL 13896)*

Half Way townsite near the Britannia mine, c. 1916. After a snow, mud and rock avalanche destroyed most of the Jane (or 1050) Camp in 1915, the Britannia Mine Company built this new townsite halfway up the mountain at what they hoped was a safer site. The homes were all identical, even to the white and green paint. *(PM)*

or Mount Sheer. It was 347 steps above the Beach townsite, but could also be reached by an aerial tramway and later by "the skip," an incline railway.

Mount Sheer developed into a thriving community for workers and their families, with a school, hospital, store, community centre and recreational facilities. A popular place among the miners, it offered numerous social activities that drew the families together and remained in place almost until the mine closed, nearly 60 years later. By 1920, 2000 people lived at the Beach and Mount Sheer townsites that made up Britannia. The community had telephone and telegraph offices and a Provincial Police constable but no other contact with the outside world except the steamships.

Surrounded by forest, mountains and water, Britannia was a wonderful location for children. They hiked the trails, fished for rock cod and picnicked at isolated beaches. They could take a boat or hike to one favourite spot with its own history, Starvation Point, just north of Britannia. The story, passed on over time by word of mouth, told of a small group of loggers who, years before, had been shipwrecked on the rocks of the point. With no trails to guide them and no boat, they almost

The Britannia Copper Mine Beach townsite, 1921. The original mill buildings (top left) were destroyed by a mill fire and flash flood later that year. *(PM)*

starved to death before some Squamish natives in a canoe came to their rescue. Today a busy highway bisects the Starvation Point area.

A short boat ride south of Britannia, the beach at Porteau Cove offered good swimming. Mr. Deeks and his family lived there in a pleasant house surrounded by a wide verandah. Visitors from Britannia could help themselves to his apples, collect nuts from his large walnut tree and picnic around a bonfire. Mr. Deeks had operated the Deeks Sand and Gravel Company since early in the 1900s, sending his laden scows to Vancouver. Deeks Creek now bears his name.

Anvil Island, not far from Britannia Beach in Howe Sound, was another favourite destination for small boat trips. Families spent enjoyable afternoons collecting Gravenstein apples from the Keelings' original orchards and visiting with Bill Champside, a property owner, and his neighbour, George Austin, a squatter. Sometimes a group of men would go by boat to the west side of the sound and visit Seaside Hotel, beside the Port Mellon pulpmill, for a cold beer and a good chin-wag.

Although life at Britannia could be idyllic, the mining community seemed destined for catastrophes. The next staggering blow hit the Beach townsite in March 1921. Fire engulfed the large wooden concentrator that dominated the south end of the town. Phyllis Malm (nee St. Laurent), the daughter of a mine employee, was 10 years old that night and the terror was still fresh in her memory over 70 years later:

I was babysitting while my parents were out, and was sitting doing my homework when the lights started to shimmer, then started going off and on. Suddenly the whole town lit up. The mill was on fire, where the Mining Museum is now. My parents always told me to get the children out if there was any problem, so I took the baby buggy outside and my parents came right away. Men were running everywhere yelling "Fire!" There was a danger of the Powder House catching fire and it was full of dynamite, so they kept hosing water onto it. They put some of the women and children into boats with blankets. I had my crucifix with me, I remember. We were out on the water all night; luckily it wasn't a bad night. Men came from Squamish and Woodfibre to help. When we got home the next morning, the fire was out but the glass in the windows of our house, facing the mill, were bubbly from the heat, and we were about four blocks from the fire.

The Britannia Mine buildings after the March, 1921 fire that destroyed the mill. Fortunately, no homes burned, although the glass in the windows of some houses bubbled from the heat. *(PM)*

Only seven months later, in October 1921, while a new steel and concrete concentrator was under construction, another disaster struck the Beach townsite. Part way up the mountain, a dam of fallen logs was holding back a lake, several acres in size, that had been expanding, unnoticed, due to very heavy rainfall. Suddenly the logs gave way and a wall of water over 20 metres (65 feet) wide and nearly 2 metres (6 feet) deep raged down Britannia Creek and swallowed up most of the homes dotting the level ground at the beach, washing them into the sound.

Hanna Swanson had moved to Britannia Beach in 1914, at the age of 6. She was 14 years old when the flood devastated the entire Beach townsite. Seventy years later she recalled:

We heard a terrible roar, like the skip [aerial tram] had gone off the track. When water started pouring through the house, my father put my mother on the dining room table, but a log came through the wall and hit the table leg. Our neighbour, Carl Berg, had a rowboat and rowed over and called to us, but couldn't get into the house. So he got a ladder and chopped a hole in the roof so we could get out and into the boat. We were taken to the manager's house—this was about midnight—and we were fed and got some clothing from the store.

Our neighbours were killed. Their house just vanished. From one house that was washed into the sound we could hear the little boys yelling. Boulders and enormous tree trunks did the worst damage.

The next day we went to Vancouver and rented housekeeping rooms because we had no house to stay in. We heard that the Famous Ladies' Clothing Store on Hastings Street was offering free dresses for lady survivors. My mother got a navy blue one, and the storekeeper thought my sister and I were big enough to have one too, although they were too long for us. The sales clerks collected money for free stockings for the children.

Fortunately the company store was one of the few buildings left standing in Britannia. It was able to provide survivors with food and clothing. The rest of the townsite was a mass of mud, trees, boulders and the wreckage of homes.

Over time, the site was cleared, houses rebuilt and the families moved back. The mine continued to produce well and the management introduced new, updated operations during the 1920s.

The aftermath of the Britannia flood, 1921. Several employees' homes were washed from the Britannia Beach townsite into Howe Sound. *(PM)*

Jim Elliott had come from the prairies looking for work in the late Depression years. In March 1937, he started at the mine and earned $5.25 a day, six days a week. He was happy to finally make such a good wage.

When I first went to Britannia, I mucked. We were supposed to shovel 16 tons [14.5 tonnes] of ore into the cars for an eight-hour shift. We just did what we could. Then I got a job on the trams, loading ore out of the chutes into ore cars.

In 1937, the townsite at the 2200-foot [670-metre] level consisted of one enormous bunkhouse that held 600 to 700 men, and two smaller ones that held 150 to 200 men each. It had a real good dry, a room where you could hang your clothes to dry separate from your [sleeping] room, have a shower in an enormous shower room, then put on your street clothes.

It was almost impossible not to be wet in the mine because water was seeping through all the time and we used water for our drills. We'd fill a 15-gallon [70 litre] tank with water and two machines would use that with air pressure for four hours' drilling. The men would come out of the mine white from the rock dust, as if they were covered with flour.

One site farther up had a ram pasture [sleeping quarters for single men] that was a series of beds three tiers high, side by side right through the place. They were muzzle-loading—you had to crawl through from the end to get into them. You hung your clothes on the end of the bed.

Miners working underground were required to wear safety hats and boots. The men wore carbide lamps on their hats to light their way in the dark tunnels. The lights contained a piece of carbide and some water. This produced a gas that the miners ignited with a flint. Jim recalled that they could write messages on the rock walls with the black from their carbide lamps. They would mark machinery with the code "B.O." for "Bad Order" to indicate when a repair was needed. Jim also remembered how impressed he was by the beautiful bright blues and reds reflected from the copper and zinc embedded in the rock.

After Jim married Alice Johnston, he and his family lived in a company house at the Mount Sheer townsite, where they enjoyed the small-town lifestyle. His daughters, Carrie, Diane and Lynda, participated in sports and joined in the yearly competition between the Beach and Mount Sheer teams. In 1958, the family moved to Squamish, where Jim later held the position of mayor.

Phyllis Malm remembered winters at this townsite on the mountainside:

We used to have 35 feet [11 metres] of snow in winter, and would walk across it right onto the tops of houses. Japanese workmen kept the wooden sidewalk shovelled, but my husband had a hard time shovelling a path from the house. He'd push at the door and shovel, push at the door and shovel, then keep shovelling until he had made a tunnel to the sidewalk.

We didn't see the sun for three months because of the shadows from the mountains, so at the beginning of winter the doctor would put up a sign in the store for the mothers to come and get the cod-liver oil for the children. We'd take long walks just to sit in the sun where it was shining.

The children wore home-made woollen coats, longjohns with woollen stockings pulled over them, and knitted hats and mittens. One day I heard Mary Dale [her daughter] crying. I ran outside and finally found her about three feet [one metre] down in the snow. She'd broken through the top crust. I had a hard time getting her out.

In the spring we'd take a trip to Vancouver and go down to the Beach site, bundled up in winter clothing, to get the steamship. The people there at sea level were in sweaters, and tulips were blooming. We'd put our galoshes in a bag and carry them with us to the city.

Through lean times and good years, the mine produced and the residents enjoyed their lifestyle until the mine closed temporarily in the 1950s and most residents moved away. In 1959 the company went into temporary liquidation. In 1963, the Anaconda Mining Company bought the property and instituted a concentrated search for new ore at Britannia. A new vein was found and with upgrading and a new market for silicon from the mill tailings, the company was able to resume operation. The mine finally closed in 1974 when the new ore reserve ran out. The area is now a national historic site.

The Pacific Great Eastern Railway

In 1906, a group of Vancouver men undertook a business enterprise that was to have a major impact, not only on the peaceful farming and ranching community of Squamish at the head of Howe Sound, but also on the province as a whole. These men decided to open a railway line from Squamish to Anderson Lake, near Lillooet. The promoters of the Howe Sound, Pemberton Valley and Northern Railway, incorporated in 1907, secretly purchased all of the navigable waterfrontage on the Squamish River—50 hectares (125 acres) of tidewater land—for the terminals and spent $25,000 on large acreages in the Cheakamus and Pemberton Valleys, a boon to the speculators who owned the land.

Highhandedly, the planners changed Squamish's name to Newport, predicting a population of up to 6000 people within five years (up from about 70 in 1900). In August 1909, amid the dust and clamour of road building and track laying, residential lots went on sale for $250 to $350; $450 to $1000 were the prices for business locations on Cleveland Avenue, the new main street. The name honoured not a pioneer, but one of the developers.

The enthusiastic directors of this new company offered glowing predictions about the town's future and the positive economic future for both small businesses and the provincial government. The rail line's original purpose was to haul logs to salt water, where new sawmills would prepare them for market. Later, speculations skyrocketed, and J.C. Keith, a prominent Vancouver businessman and a director of the company (now renamed the Howe Sound and Northern Railway, HS&NR), assured Premier Richard McBride in a letter dated January 6, 1911, that the government would derive great financial gain from the railway. Keith forecast that income from land already settled, and the settlement of land then vested in the government, would provide an increase of $50,000 per year. Timber royalties would average $2 million from the estimated 1.3 billion metres (4 billion feet) of timber in the forests between Howe Sound and Summit Lake (now Alta Lake at Whistler), and access to unused land could open up a chief source of revenue. He pointed out, "The assessment of the 210 acres [85 hectares] purchased for the purposes of the Company at the head of Howe Sound was raised from $18,000 to $140,000 and a very considerable increase made in the other lands lying in the Squamish Valley directly construction on the railway was started."

On behalf of his company, Mr. Keith was petitioning the government to guarantee interest on forthcoming HS&NR bonds, indicating governmental approval of the entire project. Until this time, the HS&NR had operated on private income.

By 1911, the company surveyors had reached Lillooet to the north. Trains using over 16 kilometres (10 miles) of track between Cheekye and tidewater were carrying 18,240 metres (60,000 feet) of logs a day from the Squamish Timber Company.[1] By April 1912, the Newport Timber Company, the largest in the area, was preparing to increase its daily shipments to 46,000 metres (150,000 feet) of lumber per day.

It's no surprise, then, that Mr. Keith and his colleagues were extremely disappointed and bitter when the provincial government passed Bill 23 in February 1912. It brought into existence the Pacific Great Eastern Railway Company (the PGE), under sole government control, replacing the HS&NR. The government named it after England's Great Eastern Railway with hopes of attracting more financial backers from that country.

Not long after passing Bill 23, the government paid close to $1,225,000 for the Howe Sound and Northern stock, rail line and townsite properties. Trials and tribulations, both financial and political, slowed the railway's development for many years.

An unusual stipulation in Bill 23 was that the government would employ only white labour on the railway. The reason for this restriction went back to the early 1880s, when the young British Columbia government twice attempted to have the Canadian House of Commons approve an act that would prevent further Chinese immigration. The majority of the politicians in the British Columbia legislature believed that the Chinese immigrants were poor coolies who tended to degrade the white labouring classes, encouraged the use of opium in the general population, and spread crime amongst themselves through their secret societies. The Canadian government was not receptive, but the provincial government's prejudice remained.

One of the first positive moves the new railway company made was to announce a competition for schoolchildren to select a more appropriate name for the town of Newport. The company sent notices of the competition on plain brown postcards to schools across British Columbia. The postcards advertised not only the opportunity for prizes, but also the fact that the government was embarking on a major enterprise to benefit the citizens of the province. Over 2000 entries flooded in, and 28 winners selected the name "Squamish," probably no surprise to the settlers. Each winner received $17.86, their portion of the $500 prize.

In 1914 the town became Squamish again, a name that was important to the Squamish people's history. They had always called their land Sko-mish, meaning "Mother of the Wind." Today a birth certificate showing Newport as the place of birth is a prized possession of some elderly Squamish residents.

The original Charter in Bill 23 called for a rail line from North Vancouver to Lillooet and Fort George (now Prince George). When surveyors and engineers reported the realities of construction costs along the rugged Howe Sound shoreline between Horseshoe Bay and Squamish, plans for that segment of line were left in abeyance for nearly 50 years. A rail line from North Vancouver's Lonsdale Avenue to Dundarave in West Vancouver did open with great fanfare on January 1, 1914, but passengers planning to continue north had to travel by steamer to Squamish in order to join up with the next section of railway. In order to provide an essential connection for passengers and freight between the end of the rail line at Squamish and Vancouver, the Union Steamship Company agreed to meet PGE trains connecting to and from the north.[2] The railway was, indeed, opening up a chief source of revenue as J.C. Keith had

Thomas Neiland's logging operation near the south end of Alta Lake, c. 1921. Neiland used horses to pull the loaded railway cars from his property to the PGE main line. Logging has been an important industry in the area since the late 1800s. J. Jardine photo. *(WMA 88.016)*

predicted to the government in 1911.

By the end of that year, passengers bumped and jostled in wooden railcars from Squamish to Alta Lake, and by early in 1915 as far as Lillooet. The line was a marvel of surveying and construction, accomplished by men without modern equipment or aerial survey methods, through terrain that had always been considered too mountainous to maintain the low grades required by a railway.

Logging camps and sawmills sprang up at points along the line, taking advantage of the accessible transport to tidewater. Between Green Lake and Alta Lake, pole cutters were the first to skid their long, straight logs to the rails. In 1926, Ross Barr and his two brothers built the area's first sawmill on Green Lake's northeast corner. Shortly after, the PGE built a station there, naming it Parkhurst after the original settlers on that land. In one period in the late 1920s, the railway picked up one carload of timber a day from the Parkhurst Mill. Other mills opened, producing timber, lumber and railroad ties.[3]

The future was not, however, to follow a smooth, even roadbed. Over the years the government suffered so many setbacks with the line that several nicknames identified the PGE: Please Go Easy, Political Government Expense, Promoters Get Everything, and Prince George—Eventually. In spite of problems, the railway did provide transportation for settlers, tourists and suppliers, as well as a means for logging companies, sawmills and miners to transport their products to a widely expanded market.[4]

Pacific Great Eastern Railway train arriving at Horseshoe Bay. It was not until 1956 that the PGE opened its service between Horseshoe Bay and Squamish, completing the rail connection from Vancouver to Prince George. *(VPL 36617)*

Due to the government's financial losses, damage from flooding, rockfalls and snowslides, and, it was suggested, political manoeuvring, the government halted further development and continued only minimal maintenance of existing services. It offered the line for sale to private purchasers in 1924, then closed the North Shore line in 1928 and had its tracks torn up except for a short stretch east of Lions Gate Bridge. The CNR used this stretch for switching. Some tracks were also torn up between Quesnel and Prince George.[5]

The slow years continued until 1949, when the incoming rail revenue topped $1,000,000 for the first time. The government decided that the line was no longer for sale and began expansion both to the north, from Quesnel, and from Horseshoe Bay to Squamish.

The route along the east shore of Howe Sound varied from precipitous cliffs to impenetrable bush bisected by deep gullies. The surveyors' only access to the site was by water taxi. Through nightmarish conditions they persevered. When construction finally began in 1954, the men faced added danger when they had to blast railbeds and four tunnels from solid rock for much of the way, as no natural grade existed on the whole route. They used more than a million kilograms of dynamite. The saga of the ill-fated railway line continued.

The last spike on the long-awaited PGE line joining Horseshoe Bay and Squamish, June 10, 1956. William H. Cunningham/*Province* photo. *(VPL 68922)*

In August 1956, great fanfare greeted the first train to arrive in Squamish from the re-opened North Vancouver station. Cheering crowds holding flags and placards surrounded the station when the train arrived, 18 hours late. One slogan read: "1912—We Started It, 1922—Rusted, 1932—Busted, 1942—Disgusted, 1956—We Made It!"

As a road along this route was still only in the early stages of construction, the trains were essential for passengers and freight now travelling from North Vancouver as far north as Prince George. The "Province's Greatest Expense" was heading into a brighter future, which included another name change—to BC Rail—in 1972.

Woodfibre Pulpmill

About 100,000 people lived in Vancouver in 1910, and more were arriving weekly. Sawmills and logging operations dotted the coast, and across Howe Sound from the Britannia Mine, a new commercial venture had its beginning on a former sawmill site at Mill Creek. The BC Sulphite Fibre

Company Ltd. began construction of the Mill Creek pulpmill, later known as Woodfibre.

The company brought workmen in by boat from Vancouver and evidently expected the men to help defray some of this expense. One early worker, Joe Williams, had come from England looking for work in Vancouver when jobs were scarce. He recalled having difficulty finding a job, as most of the signs along Hastings Street in Vancouver read "No Englishmen need apply." One day he saw an advertisement for the new Mill Creek pulpmill. The mill wanted men if they were willing to pay a fee of $1. Joe Williams was, and did, and worked for the company for many years.

The workers constructed a dock. They cleared the forest and, among its stumps, built bunkhouses for the employees, then began laying the foundations of British Columbia's third coastal pulpmill. Two tall, wooden structures and a long, low building reaching to the waterfront were set in a clearing bordered by the forest and Howe Sound. Two years later, the first pulp went over the number one pulp machine. The company was in business.

As the number of employees grew and families joined them, the cookhouses and bachelor bunkhouses became inadequate. The need to develop a formal townsite was evident. By 1917, the company had built white frame homes on the Lower and Upper North Hill, and a row bordered what was to become the playing field. In those days the houses were not insulated, and early residents remember the cold Squamish winds blowing through the cracks.

Whalen Pulp and Paper Mills purchased the mill in 1917, continued to develop its capacity, and added more residences. During these early times the mill had its own sawmill, which cut logs brought in by tugs. The logs were cut into cants, 1.5-metre (4- to 5-foot) boards, that were then put through the chipper to provide woodchips for the pulp operation. Five shingle machines also started production in 1919.

The community was geographically isolated, but regular Union Steamship service offered a three-hour trip to or from Vancouver, and a small ferry from Horseshoe Bay connected the residents to the outside world. A horse-drawn cart carried the mail, milk and groceries from the ship to the store where housewives could purchase essentials and pick up mail at the post office, operated between 1920 and 1923 by J. Macindoe. As another post office in BC already had the name Mill Creek, in 1921

A view of Woodfibre pulpmill from the Lower Townsite, c. 1938. The digester building is at centre. *(BCARS HP97378)*

Mill Creek became Woodfibre, a new name selected through a school competition. Cathy Haar won a $50 prize for her idea.

Woodfibre's population of 500 had schools, Roman Catholic and Anglican churches, a government telegraph office, and later a hospital. Dr. C.G. McLean was kept busy providing medical assistance to injured workmen and dealing with family illnesses. He probably accompanied the men who rowed across the sound to Britannia Beach to provide aid after the fire and flood in 1921.

George Scott's Mill Creek Lumber Co. Ltd. operated close by and supplied logs to the pulpmill. About two kilometres (one mile) up the mountain, Cedar Creek Logging ran a sawmill, used horses to haul logs and sent shingle bolts down a flume to the sound.

The Henriette Lake Dam, constructed on the mountain high above the shore, provided a necessary water reservoir for the Woodfibre residents and a continuous supply of fresh water to the mill operations.

Whalen Pulp and Paper went into receivership in 1923, but the future of the business looked bright in 1925 when BC Pulp and Paper Co. Ltd. took over the assets. The new owners modernized many operations and added new facilities. Barkers were installed to remove bark from the logs,

The Woodfibre pulpmill North Hill Townsite, c. 1945. The townsite included a school (at left) and a playing field (centre). *(PM)*

the pulpmill dock was enlarged, and a new warehouse, small boat float and passenger dock were constructed.

As the mill expanded, more employees and their families enjoyed the lifestyle at the townsite. Many said that it was "the best place in the world to live." They never had to lock their doors or worry for their children's safety. A bowling alley, swimming pool, community centre and ball teams provided recreational activities. The residents were proud of their gardens and held contests to choose the most attractive ones.

The company, however, experienced many setbacks including strikes, rockfalls and floods. In 1955, a huge underwater slide undermined the dock pilings and swept them far out into the Sound. The entire dock and adjoining warehouse collapsed, and 1270 tonnes (1400 tons) of pulp and five fork trucks disappeared into the water.

After several shutdowns in the 1950s, the result of various mechanical problems and a strike, and with improved access to and from Squamish, many families moved across the water to that town, leaving nearly half of the homes in Woodfibre unoccupied. The plant expanded, but the need for a townsite declined. During the 1960s, the company demolished most of the houses, and employees commuted on a ferry from Darrell Bay, south of Squamish. A pack of nearly 200 cats grew from pets left behind, and the company had to call in the SPCA to remove them.

Woodfibre has continued to expand and now produces kraft pulp, which is shipped to high-grade paper mills for use in the production of quality paper. Current production levels average 730 tonnes (800 tons) of kraft pulp per day which is shipped around the world. Today's modern, highly automated plant faces the ghost of Britannia Mines across the sound.

The Pulpmill at Port Mellon

While Mill Creek Pulp and Paper Mill (Woodfibre) experienced its first growing pains, Pioneer Mills, halfway down Howe Sound's western coast on the way to Gibson's Landing, had already begun its uncertain future. Captain Henry A. Mellon purchased 32 hectares (80 acres) of land for $6500 from George Cates and began construction of a pulpmill on the level stretch of ground just south of Rainy River, with forest to the west and a marshy foreshore. The location had most of the basic requirements for a mill: access to water-generated power from the mountain creeks, a nearby forest for timber, and tidewater for transportation of coal, machinery, logs and workers. It was close to an abandoned Squamish village, Khay-Kul-Hun, which, according to August Jack Khahtsahlano, was formerly home to about 40 people.

Pioneer Mills began production on October 14, 1909. Its major product was coloured wrapping paper. The owners believed there was a large enough market in Vancouver to make their mill profitable. Unfortunately, this did not prove to be an accurate projection. Four months after the mill produced its first paper, it had its first shutdown. Costs were higher and demand lower than expected.

Mill Creek pulpmill just up the coast continued to enlarge its facilities and employ more men, but the Pioneer Mill stayed closed for seven long years, visited only by a caretaker who lived at the Seaside Hotel, across Rainy River from the mill.

When Rainy River Pulp and Paper Company took over in 1917 with 65 employees, it began to produce kraft pulp, but no paper. The lure of jobs brought some men from Gibson's Landing. With no real bunkhouses, they slept anywhere they could find room to set up beds. An old metal building on the beach acted as cookhouse at a site that was untidy and rundown. Later, management built a boarding house and began improvements to existing buildings.

Optimism for the future was short-lived. After two years the Rainy River mill went bankrupt again, and then again after a five-year production run between 1920 and 1925 under the ownership of Western Canada Pulp and Paper Company.[6]

Problems beset all of the large businesses that had developed around Howe Sound since 1900, but the pulpmill at Rainy River seemed to suffer most. When new owners took over in 1925, they could not have known the Great Depression was looming on the horizon and the price of kraft pulp was to drop drastically. This time the closure lasted until 1935, after which conditions improved and a townsite developed. For the first time, residents of the local communities, including Gibson's Landing, were able to realize a steady income and many moved to new homes on company property. Better times looked to be there to stay— until 1949, when the mill closed down again due to low market prices.

Oji Paper of Japan purchased the mill for $635 million in December 1987. They officially took over the mill April 1, 1988, creating the new Howe Sound Pulp and Paper Ltd., and began renovations which included meeting government standards for pollution reduction. Today the giant

The mill at Port Mellon, north of Gibsons on the west shore of Howe Sound, in 1912. The business was one of British Columbia's first pulpmills. It experienced severe financial setbacks for many years, but is still in operation today. *(EPM)*

Howe Sound Pulp and Paper mill at Port Mellon exudes an aura of prosperity. Its problem-beset history is well buried under the modern buildings and wharves and the misty effluent from its stacks.

Seaside Hotel

Ironically, a very profitable business, the Seaside Hotel, operated continuously just across Rainy River from the mill. Andrew Jackson Cates and his son, Captain Charles Cates, founder of a towing company in North Vancouver, had purchased land in 1894. Their land was at the shore, beside a river that was called Cates Creek at the time. It had been the site of a minor gold rush in 1891. Another son, George Cates, a shipbuilder, bought out his father in 1903 and started to build the Seaside Hotel in 1909, the same year that construction began on Pioneer Mills. The hotel became a popular picnic and holiday centre, and while the pulpmill staggered through its shutdowns and problems, boatloads of holidayers made the resort a valuable enterprise.

The hotel and beach were a focal point for Howe Sound residents, attracting families of picnickers who arrived in small boats from Britannia, Squamish, Woodfibre and Gibson's Landing. Captain Cates purchased the SS *St. Ann* and the SS *Port Mellon Flyer* specially to transport Vancouver tourist groups to Seaside. In the 1920s, Union steamships carried groups as large as 200 people from the Howe Sound communities and the city for company and church picnics at Rainy River.

Well-dressed men, sporting their straw boaters, and women, stylishly attired and topped by their cloche hats, carried ashore picnic baskets stuffed with typical picnic fare—potato salad, pork and beans, hard boiled eggs and chicken. The children raced ahead to lay claim to picnic tables under the trees. Tug-of-war, races, swimming events and hikes up the shore of Rainy River into the lush forest added to the day's excitement. The men could cool down with a cold beer at the hotel's bar.

A fire destroyed the hotel in 1933. The Cateses sold the land to a Mr. Storey who rebuilt the hotel and operated it until 1951, when Canadian Forest Products took it over. The *Coast News* of November 27, 1958, reported another fire, which destroyed the top storey.

The hotel was restored in 1959, but closed in the 1960s due to a lack of business. The cafeteria remained open and was used as a conference room until the 1980s, when the building was torn down. The Howe Sound

The Seaside Hotel, just across Rainy River from the Port Mellon pulpmill on Howe Sound. Union Steamships vessels and the *Port Mellon Flyer*, the passenger ferry shown at left, brought visitors for overnight stays and group picnics. The hotel was a very popular tourist destination. *(CVA OUT P1117 N660)*

Pulp and Paper Mill expanded across Rainy River, added fill to the site, changing the shoreline, and built mill equipment that covered the hotel's former location.

Steamships and Resorts

Of all the businesses, large and small, that appeared in Sea to Sky Country in the early 1900s, there is no doubt that the steamship companies—Union Steamship and Terminal Steamship—had the greatest impact upon the cohesion and development of the emerging settlements.

The Union Steamship Company served the settlers, logging camps and sawmills up and down British Columbia's coast from 1889 onward. Isolated communities looked forward to the whistle from the arriving *Leonora*, the *Senator* or the *Skidegate*, and early settlers told many stories about their trips on the *Cutch* and *Comox*.

The Cates family, all five brothers master mariners, were also familiar to families living on Howe Sound or travelling north from Squamish to the interior. Captain John Cates' first steamer, the wooden *Defiance*,

ferried settlers to their land before 1900. He formed the Terminal
Steamship Co. Ltd. in 1902 (later the Terminal Steam Navigation Co.
Ltd.). His brother George's shipyard on False Creek built one of the settlers' favourite vessels, the *Britannia*, in 1902. She was to serve the Howe
Sound communities for many years and was the first of the Terminal
Company's many passenger steamers. A handsome wooden vessel with a
capacity of 300 passengers, she was considered to be the best day-trip
ship out of Vancouver. She had a promenade deck and a dining room
where waiters, formally attired in black and white with a linen napkin
over one arm, served three-course meals. Rows of seats, upholstered in
maroon plush velvet, were usually filled with passengers—excited children making their rare visits to the big city of Vancouver, mothers on
yearly shopping trips for family clothing, new settlers nervously examining the rugged country that would become their new home, and tourists
simply enjoying the boat ride, the mountains and the sparkling water.
The hold held everything from live chickens to orange crates. The toot of
the *Britannia*'s whistle was a welcome signal to isolated pioneers who
looked forward to the weekly visits when she would drop off mail and

The Terminal steamship *Britannia*, docking at Snug Cove, Bowen Island, c. 1905.
Launched in 1902, the ship was popular with campers and picnickers visiting the
island, and it also made many stops at settlements and logging camps around Howe
Sound. It later became a Union steamship. *(BIH 43/VPL 2882)*

supplies, and bring news from the city.

After John Cates purchased the Mannion property on Bowen Island in 1900, he became interested in developing another business enterprise: a first-class picnic, camping and hotel resort on the island. It would, of course, be served by his busy little steamers, which daily left Evans, Coleman and Evans wharf in Vancouver on Burrard Inlet. After he added the *Britannia* to his fleet, large group picnics of over 300 people could spend the day at what Captain Cates called Terminal Farm. He offered meals and lodging at Joseph Mannion's former home, exotically renamed Hotel Monaco, its wide verandah looking out over Hotel Bay. Cates bought more land, cleared the forest, and opened the new Terminal Hotel. A farm with a dairy herd, chickens and gardens provided fresh milk, meat, eggs and produce for campers and the hotel's kitchens. A 147.5-hectare (364-acre) park with a lagoon, Japanese tea garden, dance pavilion, general store and telephone service to Vancouver enticed picnickers and overnight or weekly guests who could enjoy the hotel's "Home Comforts" for $14 weekly or $2.20 daily. Later he added cottages for weekly renters.

The Cates' business enterprises were successful and popular, but in December 1920, Captain John Cates gave up the life of a resort and steamship fleet owner and sold his assets to the Union Steamship Company, which continued to develop the Bowen Island tourist destination and the steamship service in Howe Sound waters.

For more than 30 years, the Union Steamship Company held the government franchise for ferry service to Snug Cove on Bowen Island, where its extremely popular resort attracted thousands of visitors yearly. Moonlight cruises, company picnics, camping grounds, cottages and Mount Strahan Lodge (the newly renovated and renamed Terminal Hotel) drew crowds from Vancouver. They enjoyed a saltwater swimming pool, tennis, horseback riding and hiking through a woodland setting. Saturday night "booze cruises" became infamous. A new, large general store, designed in Tudor style and built near the Snug Cove ferry dock, provided necessary provisions. It still stands today and is used for the post office and government offices. The company's holdings reached 526 hectares (1300 acres), and its coffers overflowed.

After Lions Gate Bridge opened in 1939 and made the North Shore accessible to cars, Union Steamship purchased Whytecliff Park resort, on the mainland near Horseshoe Bay. The company established a ferry service to Bowen Island from a cove at the south end of Whytecliff Park and encouraged tourists to make the faster trip by car and a short ferry ride.

Times were changing, however, as roads opened up the interior and people chose to explore by car rather than travel on the less versatile ferries. Although the company made attempts to rejuvenate the resort on Bowen Island—renamed Evergreen Park in 1956—the hotel closed one year later and was finally demolished in 1962. The ferry to Whytecliff was cancelled. Many cottages were sold for one dollar each to people who could move them to a new location.

Bowen Island's only major business was no more, a segment of history remaining only in the memories of those who had been part of the great excursions and those Bowen Islanders who had chosen the quiet island life, but had shared it with their renowned neighbour, the Union Steamship Company resort.

CHAPTER 8

THE SEQUESTERED LIFE

Most of Father's later life was spent on this property, where he had a comfortable home constructed and surrounded himself with a lovely garden in which was an artificial lake. For a number of years he raised canaries, pheasants and Belgian hares, and kept deer in a nearby enclosure. His hobby was the growing of lilies-of-the-valley and violets.

—Miss Elsa Wiegand, speaking about her father Charles' home on Gambier Island, in an interview with Major J.S. Matthews on December 27, 1946

Anvil Island

Every evening, in his one-bedroom cabin by the shore on Anvil Island, George Austin would put on his headphones, blocking out the constant wash of the waves, and twirl the knobs on his battery-powered radio until the news came through clearly. He liked to make notes of the important events of the day to share with the other two bachelors who lived near him on the isolated island. Earlier in his life he had fished and logged around Howe Sound. Now he was an oldtimer with no evident means of support, but he always had a large vegetable garden, and his friends from Britannia would bring him food. He was very well read, but depended on his Britannia friends to bring him reading material.

Tall, lanky Bill Champside, his neighbour, had moved to Anvil Island from the Maritimes after the First World War. By that time, most of the buildings belonging to the two brickyards on the island had burnt down, leaving only concrete foundations. Bill moved into his home on the former brickyard property, surrounded it with a huge vegetable garden, and continued to develop the productive orchard that Thomas Keeling had established in the 1890s. He welcomed the two Englishmen, George Dowell and George Austin, who lived close by.

George Dowell, a hermit, was content in his one-room beachside shack just west of his friend George Austin. Even though he had a hook for a hand on one arm, he was a talented carpenter and built boats for several residents around the Sound.

A small group of men would cross by boat from Britannia on weekends, bringing groceries and a bottle of liquor. Albin Granlund was a regular and Carl Berg also joined the group at times. (He was the man who rescued Hanna Swanson and her family with his rowboat in the Britannia flood of 1921.) The parties became lively after a few drinks; Albin would sing "O sole mio," and there would be a sing-along. George Austin would often accompany the Britannia men by boat across to the Seaside Hotel at Rainy River where they would sit in the beer parlour sharing stories with the locals.

Marie Kendall was six years old in 1928 when her family first rent-

Albin Granlund, a Britannia Beach resident, visiting George Austin at his two-room waterfront house on Anvil Island, c. 1945. *(MK)*

ed a cottage from Mrs. Atkinson on Anvil for the summer holidays. Two or three years later, having fallen in love with their captivating island retreat, her mother Ida bought three hectares (seven acres) on the southwest corner of the island from Bill Champside, and built a home. Later they built another, smaller house on another three hectares of adjoining Crown land. They called this one "The Little House." Lumber, granite blocks and building supplies were barged from Vancouver.

Marie recalled 65 years later: "We had grocery orders come up on the Union steamship from Woodward's store in Vancouver. The ship called in Tuesday mornings and Thursday afternoons, and we'd go out on Bill Champside's boat, *The Gull*, to unload our supplies, including the mail, which he distributed from his house. His living room was the post office. Mr. Wiegand, who lived on Gambier Island across from us, used to row over to Anvil Island to get his mail. His daughter, Elsa, was a school teacher and used to be up there in the summer with him. There was

George Dowell outside his one-room beach shack on Anvil Island, c. 1945. Dowell lived as a hermit for many years. Although he lost one arm while serving in the navy during the First World War, he built his own small boat and later renovated a tug. Eventually he moved into the tug, and tied up at the Seaside Hotel wharf near Port Mellon. *(MK)*

another oldtimer named Bill Baines who lived on the mainland by McNab Creek near Port Mellon, who also rowed over to Anvil for his mail."

Since there was no electricity, they used coal oil lanterns. Marie's mother cooked on a woodstove, kept the butter in a crock of salt water, and used canned milk. The spring where they got their drinking water would dry up in the summer, and Marie used to hike to the boundary between their land and Mrs. Atkinson's property to collect pails of water. A tall rock face there was continuously wet with water that dripped from above through the maidenhair ferns that grew in the clefts. Marie's mother had set a tin tub on the ground under this rock face, and Marie scooped pails of the water that had dripped into the tub.

She still retains wonderful, happy memories of her early life of freedom on Anvil Island. With no one else around for company, Bill Champside became her dear friend. She spent most of her time helping him around his house and garden and going with him in his boat to Britannia and Woodfibre to sell his Gravenstein apples and sacks of corn. She helped make apple cider and build a picket fence and a boat, and learned how to make cedar shakes.

"It was one of the saddest day of my life when he died," she reminisced. She was 14 years old that Christmas of 1936, and remembers George Austin and George Dowell building a rough wooden coffin for the body. Carrying it down the long flight of steps to the beach, through the snow, and lifting it into the launch was an exhausting effort.

George Austin took over the post office in January 1937, and the

Champside property was sold to the Steeves family, who had previously owned property on Keats Island. The land later became the site of Daybreak Point Bible Camp.

After their mother died in 1962, Marie and her sister sold their property to Dr. Ken Morton who, in the early 1990s, sold it to the Killam family. Today, several families own recreational land around the point on each side of the church camp.

Gambier Island

Just south of Anvil Island, Gambier Island's forested shores—especially around West, Centre and Long Bays (dubbed "Three Bays" by early settlers)—attracted loggers for many years. During the early 1900s, Lee, Thorne and Johnson Lumber Mill operated on the east side of West Bay. It hired men for heavy work, also giving them the opportunity to

Bill Champside, Anvil Island, 1929. He moved to the island in the 1920s, became the postmaster, farmed his land and grew fruit. He sold his produce to residents of Britannia and the neighbouring islands. *(MK)*

enjoy a social life after hours. The mill had a boarding house, but also, perhaps more importantly, a hotel with licensed premises, unusual at such an isolated camp.

Joe Mitchel, the first white child born on the island, at Long Bay, in 1892, recalled watching the handloggers from his family's home on West Bay when he was young. After felling one of the giant firs or cedars, the men would hitch it to a small boat and row across the bay, towing the tree behind. Collecting their fee from the sawmill owner, their next stop would be the hotel bar where they would drink up their pay and head off tipsily in search of another suitable tree.

From 1918 to 1925, seven timber companies operated on Gambier Island. During the 1920s, the water of the island's bays, especially West, Centre and Long Bays, became the site of a flourishing business—log

John Lewis Hudson, a logger, cutting cordwood on Gambier Island, 1906. He would cut the large fir log (right) into rounds (left), then split the rounds into cordwood. (*VPL 4995*)

booming. Since the late 1880s, tugs had been towing large booms of logs directly to the mills on Burrard Inlet, False Creek and the Fraser River. These large mills needed a back-up supply of logs to maintain operations over the winter months when the more northerly logging camps closed down. They also sometimes needed logs to fill special orders. It became too expensive to maintain storage at their mill sites, so the towing companies began setting up their own log-booming grounds in sheltered coves. There they would break up the booms and sort the logs by species and grade, then sell them to the mills. Preston-Mann used West Bay, Pacific Coyle Centre Bay, and Young & Gore and M.R. Cliff together located at Long Bay. These tug owners were among the most active log towers on the coast.[1] The work required to sort and maintain the log booms provided employment for several local men. As well, Gambier Island's booms became a favourite spot for boaters to tie up overnight.

Logging practices have changed dramatically in the last few years.

A logging operation at Port Graves on Long Bay, Gambier Island, 1905. This steam donkey was probably the first one used on Howe Sound and was still in operation during the 1930s. Throughout this period, logging was a profitable activity. *(EPM 143)*

West Bay was a sorting area where logs were graded, then towed to mills. Now most log-sort areas are on dry land and West Bay no longer stores logs. Many log booms are now "bundle booms," bundles of logs cabled together at a dry land sort, then dumped into the water for towing. They take up less water space than the flat booms. Mills now order timber on an as-needed basis, so there is not the need to store logs for long periods. A few towing firms still own water leases around Gambier Island for storing logs in the water, but there is much less wood kept there than in previous years.

More important to the island's future, in the early 1900s some settlers were building permanent homes around the shoreline, and a gradual influx of summer residents began to camp on the shores of sheltered bays and on open headlands with magnificent views. Probably these people preferred a more isolated setting than the easier to reach but busier camping grounds on Bowen Island.

Charles Thompson took his family by steamer for their first visit to Gambier in 1903. They loved the island life and returned every summer. Eventually they purchased land on West Bay at the old sawmill site. They

A forestry scaler at work. Scalers graded logs in log booms, recording the size and type of wood, before the logs were sent on to sawmills or pulpmills. *(VPL 37692)*

fixed up the deserted bunkhouse for a shelter, whitewashed it inside and out, and divided the long room into four bedrooms by hanging sheets from wires that ran across the ceiling. A rustic verandah fronted the building. In the lean-to kitchen, Mrs. Thompson kept a big ham and bacon hanging behind the woodstove. Mildred Ridley, their daughter, later remembered how she and the other children would row to Centre Bay to collect pails of water from an old mine excavation. As was the case with many of the summer residents, father worked during the week and visited his family on the weekends, travelling with other fathers on the steamer *Britannia*, one of the "Daddy Boats."

Bonfires on the shore were a favourite evening pastime, and neighbours rowed over to join in the fun and share some fresh fish cooked over the embers.

Some of the permanent residents developed farms both for their own food and also for the income from the sale of their produce. Arthur Davies' 158-hectare (390-acre) farm at the head of Long Bay provided many varieties of fruit and vegetables, some of which he sold in Vancouver, often rowing the boxes of produce there in a small boat. Cows and sheep also roamed his fields and orchards. He sold his property in the early 1900s to a Mr. McFeely, one of the partners in a hardware firm in Vancouver, who planted 1100 more fruit trees and added Jersey cattle and a large barn. The farm was a showplace.

Thomas Austin pre-empted a lot on the southwest side of the island in 1905 and named his location New Brighton after his former home in England. He lived there for 44 years. (Today New Brighton is the site of a small general store and the dock for a small ferry that runs regularly between Gambier and Langdale, near Gibsons.)

In 1910, 58-year-old Charles Lett and his wife bought 5 hectares (13 acres) of land at Grace (now Gambier) Harbour, at the southwest corner of West Bay. They were among the early permanent residents attracted by the serenity and beauty. The Letts built a three-storey home that nestled in the encircling forest, overlooking Bowen Island and Howe Sound's eastern shore. They had a small farm and enjoyed the community spirit developing in the small group of settlers.

The idyllic life was not without its dangers. Forest fires were a constant threat to the wooden houses, and in 1923 the Letts' home burned to the ground. The couple struggled to remove some belongings. Alone and homeless, they slept the night in the barn and the next day managed to signal a passing boat. The intense heat had damaged Mr. Lett's lungs and he died a few days later. In spite of this tragedy, the Letts' love of the island passed down through the family to the fifth generation. Relatives still own the land and spend countless happy hours there.

As Gambier's permanent population increased rapidly between 1900 and 1925, mail delivery became a necessity. A travelling post office brought welcome mail to the residents. Robert Turner was purser on the SS *Britannia* and would literally drop the mail off the deck to whoever rowed out to catch it. The island's first post office opened at Gambier's southeast corner, Hope Point, in 1908, and the second in 1919 at New Brighton.

Enough children lived near Long Bay to need a school, which opened at Hope Point in 1915. After 1920 it closed and the students travelled by boat to school at Gibson's Landing.

Children growing up in the secluded settings scattered around the sound enjoyed the whole outdoors as their playground. The reminiscences of Nicol Warn are typical. He and his sister and two brothers spent their childhood on the beaches, in the fields and forest, and on the ocean around their home near the waterfront tidal flats at the end of Gambier's Long Bay. Nicol was born in 1943—very nearly in the water taxi his father and mother, Jack and Joan, were taking to Vancouver General Hospital for his birth.

The Warn family had bought a 146-hectare (360-acre) farm from Mr. McFeely about 1935. The land was originally pre-empted by Arthur Davies and William Johnson in the 1880s. Jack's brother and his wife, Bill and Polly Warn, and the Warn brothers' parents had homes there also. Nicol recalled the pleasures of his boyhood:

Gambier Store and Post Office at Gambier Harbour (previously Grace Harbour), Gambier Island, c. 1930. The store was originally operated by Arthur Lett, who rowed to isolated homes along the shore delivering groceries. H. McCall photo. *(EPM C72)*

We spent all summer in the water—we could swim like fish, waded in the tidal pools searching for sea life, and, when we were old enough, explored the shoreline in canoes, a sailboat and rowboats, and on logs and rafts. We never got enough of the water.

Just south of what is now the public float is a gravelly beach with a big rock we used to call "Gibraltar." We searched hour upon hour along that beach for broken Indian arrow heads. The Indians must have chipped points there and discarded them when they broke. We used to find all sorts of things. I had quite a large pouch of them at one time. The tugs out in front of the beach used to stir up the mud and unearth piles of clam shells, probably an Indian shellfish steaming pit or a very small midden.

They were constantly building things—rafts, forts, carved animals—and sometimes would "go native," painting themselves up with blackberry juice and the blue clay common on the island. The old cedar stumps left over from the early logging operations were enormous—sometimes about three metres (ten feet) across at the base. Sometimes the interior had rotted away and the children could crawl inside and make cool, damp, cedar-scented secret forts. Nicol says, "I believe a Mr. Iverson at Port Mellon actually had a cedar stump house."

When summer was over, the realities of school life replaced many fun-filled hours. Joan Warn had been a teacher, and the three older children attended home school around the kitchen table. Farm chores were always waiting to take up time, with horses, cows, pigs, sheep, ducks, geese and chickens to care for. Nicol remembers earning his first money picking apples in their orchard. The family sold fruit to jam factories in Vancouver.

Although they sometimes accompanied their father when he transported livestock in the boat, every year they knew for sure they would have two special visits to Vancouver—a trip to the PNE (Pacific National Exhibition) in August and a Christmas shopping trip in December. Nicol remembers the strong currents under Lions Gate Bridge and seeing the dorsal fins of what they called "blackfish" (killer whales).

The family would travel by boat to pick up mail and supplies at Drage's post office and store at Gambier Harbour, but later had to go as far as Gibson's Landing for their mail.

Their main social group was their extended family, but they would have visits from tugboat skippers and workers on the log booms. Some neighbours, like Joe Mitchel and his family, lived along the shore nearby. Nicol's mother enjoyed chatting with a woman who occasionally visited to sell sundries from her boat.

After Nicol had completed grade six at home, his parents felt it was time for a public school education, so when he was twelve years old the family moved to Roberts Creek, north of Gibson's Landing on the Sunshine Coast. Thus began a new life, but even now Nicol can hear in his memories the welcome sound of the Union Steamship whistle as the boat arrived at the dock with their mail-order supplies.

Today, his lifelong love of the natural environment is evident in his choice of home. Although not on Gambier Island, it is only a few kilometres away on secluded forested land on the Sunshine Coast. The windows overlooking a rushing creek are set into two walls that meet in a V, like a ship's prow.

The Warns no longer live on the island, but today there are many full- and part-time residents who enjoy the seclusion and natural beauty.

Because the only road winds through the heavily treed and rocky land of the island's southwest corner, the communities, including one recreational subdivision, on other parts of the island are fairly separate, but all the residents are united in their commitment to protect the natural environment on Gambier.

Horseshoe Bay

Southeast of Gambier, Horseshoe Bay's forested crescent of shoreline was interrupted in only one location by the early years of this century. A small red cabin sat alone among the trees on the southeast corner. Edward (Scotty) Wishart had settled there in 1895 and set up a logging operation. By 1909, his logging days were over and he received few visitors at his isolated home.

The surrounding property, then known as White Cliff City (now Horseshoe Bay), also included White Cliff Point, the promontory around the southwest corner that was named by a British Admiralty survey team in the 1800s. Colonel Albert Whyte and Sir Charles Tupper, Vancouver aldermen, were two directors of the company that purchased the 526 hectares (1300 acres) of land—all except for Wishart's holding—in the name of the West Shore and Northern Land Company Ltd., divided it into 16-metre (50-foot) lots and, in July 1909, formally opened it as a summer resort, accessible only by water.

One day in about 1910, a boat carrying six children and their parents nosed in to shore. The Roedde family from Vancouver was looking for a summer retreat and were excited when they discovered the scenic cove with a safe anchorage for their boat, as Admiralty charts showed the bay as only a slight indentation in the coastline. Exploring the woods and shoreline, they knew they had found their Shangri-la.

The Roeddes purchased two lots at the southwest corner, the location that Sewell's Landing and Marina later occupied. Their task of building a summer home presented many problems—there was no road access and there was thick underbrush and giant trees. After bringing in a man by boat from Vancouver to blast out stumps, they cleared a site, then towed in a three-room, pre-cut house on a scow. The first summer home in Horseshoe Bay echoed to the sound of happy voices.

While the Pacific Great Eastern (PGE) Railway was laying tracks from North Vancouver to Horseshoe Bay, Colonel Whyte approached the company with a request to name the Horseshoe Bay station "Whytecliff,"

spelled the same way as his own name. The park on the height of land
south of the bay still bears that name. The first PGE train rolled into
Whytecliff Station in 1914, and although the engine could only crawl up
some grades, the area was now more accessible and many people built
summer residences there. A hotel, dance hall and tea rooms brought
commerce to the burgeoning little community.

Lew Hall used to meet the trains, packed with picnickers and
campers, with Horseshoe Bay's first taxi, his Chevrolet 490 touring car. He
would charge 15 cents for the trip to the beach. In 1918, the West
Vancouver Municipal Council published a pamphlet extolling the community's virtues: "A few minutes' walk from Whytecliff station is Horseshoe
Bay, the gem set into Whytecliff townsite, comprising over 1,200 acres
[486 hectares] of natural grandeur in horseshoe design around the rip-
pling waters, only divided by a generous fringe of enticing beach." They
encouraged visitors to come to the free parkland that had a bath house,
refreshment pavilion, picnic tables and swings for the children.

Early in the 1920s, the first of many ferries began a service from a
pier on Horseshoe Bay to Bowen Island. It carried passengers who had
travelled by PGE from North Vancouver. John H. Brown, founder of the

The Horseshoe Bay townsite, August 1936. This was a popular fishing and picnicking
spot, and visitors were also attracted by the teahouse and hotel. (*VPL 10291*)

Sannie Transportation Company ferry, 1940. Tommy White ran the company from 1922 to 1954, providing ferry services to passengers from Horseshoe Bay to points around Howe Sound, especially picnickers and campers heading for Bowen Island. The boats also regularly delivered groceries to property owners at Hood Point, Bowen Island. *(BIH #534)*

Sannie Transportation Company Limited, named his business after an Australian racehorse upon which he had placed a successful wager. Tommy White took over the business in 1922 and continued the service to and from Bowen Island, providing day-trip service for visitors and residents for 25 cents each way. Lions Gate Bridge had not yet been constructed across the entrance to Burrard Inlet, and the only alternative for Bowen residents wishing to visit Vancouver was to travel via the Union steamships. The steamships usually made one trip per day, meaning that the visit had to include an overnight stay in town.

The "Sannies" were very popular and became part of many happy memories. The crew would deliver the Vancouver *Sun* and *Province* newspapers, sometimes the mail, pass on messages by telephone to Vancouver, and even drop off groceries. The property owners in the new Hood Point Estates, on the northeast corner of Bowen Island, could reach

Bill Davies' store at Snug Cove only by a difficult trail, so the Sannies made special stops at the cottages so the crew could pick up grocery orders, leave them at Snug Cove, pick up the groceries later, and deliver them in the "grocery boat" daily during July and August. The boat's arrival became the social occasion of the day. The Sannies also ferried passengers from Horseshoe Bay for excursions to other destinations around Howe Sound.

In 1928, when the PGE closed its rail line from North Vancouver, buses would carry passengers to the bay along Marine Drive, which had been extended as far west as Horseshoe Bay that year.

Also during the 1920s, C. Howard Rodgers opened the first gasoline barge at Horseshoe Bay and started a water taxi service that could carry about 12 people per trip. Anyone wishing to visit any point on Howe Sound could arrange for unscheduled "taxi" service. Rodgers' boat also carried patients to hospital in emergency situations. The fierce Squamish winds in winter could tear out his floats in the bay, so he had to tow them around the northwest point of Horseshoe Bay, south into Fisherman's Cove for winter storage.

In 1931 Dan Sewell moved to Horseshoe Bay with his wife, Eva, and two sons Art and Tom. He purchased the former Roedde summer home, which had been sold to the Thorpes, and re-opened it as a hotel, calling it Whytecliff Lodge. It had a dining room, a store and sleeping accommodation upstairs. The Sewells then began to construct floats and built boats that they offered for hire. This was the beginning of the well-known Sewell's Landing and Marina, which has attracted thousands of fishermen over the years. Movie stars and politicians also discovered it and passed the word around to their associates.

Another man whose business became a landmark moved to Horseshoe Bay in 1946. Joe Troll opened his first fish and chip stand, and mostly due to his love of people and gregarious personality, he attracted customers and later expanded to Troll's Restaurant, still a central fixture in the community, now operated by his son.

After the Lions Gate Bridge was completed in 1938, car traffic increased to the North Shore, and the Union Steamship Company purchased the property at Whytecliff Park. Besides offering cottage rentals and a tearoom, the company built a ferry landing float at the south end of the bay and expanded service from there to Bowen Island on first the *Comox*, then the *Bowen*, with parking space available at the park. This service offered some competition to the Sannies, but did not make a serious difference to their income. However, in 1944 the Union Steamship Company purchased Tommy White's shares in the Sannie Transportation Company but retained him as manager and maintained this popular Horseshoe Bay and Whytecliff ferry service for foot passengers.

Because of transportation restrictions during the Second World War, Union Steamship discontinued the dining room and ferry service and leased the buildings to a boys' school for a period of time. Later the company sold residential properties there and reinstated the tourist service. In 1952, the ferry service was discontinued from Whytecliff at the end of the summer.

Brunswick Beach

Bowen Island's successful summer resort must have encouraged development of other beach property close by on the mainland shore. On April 24, 1909, the Vancouver *Province* advertised that Bishop Brothers Real Estate was selling lots at "Vancouver's New Pleasure Resort" located on Brunswick Beach, one hour and fifteen minutes from Vancouver by steamer or pleasure launch. The land, on Howe Sound's eastern shore just north of what would later become the village of Lions Bay, had been surveyed into about 300 lots, some on the water but most on the hillside. In reality, many of the lots were inaccessible due to rock bluffs and creek beds. The real estate was put on the market for as little as one dollar down and one dollar per week for a $100 lot.

The developer included about 40 lots in a row along the shoreline and on the rocky point of land that juts out into the water. South of the point is Alberta Bay, and the southern section of the development lined its shore. These were the only lots that ever sold.

Mature evergreens crowded the shoreline and covered the slopes leading to Harvey Mountain behind and Brunswick Mountain to the north. The mountain had been named after HMS *Brunswick*, one of the ships that had been in Britain's "Glorious First of June" battle with France. This was virgin land, formerly used only by native people, probably as an overnight stopping place on canoe trips. August Jack Khahtsahlano said that it was called Kul-ate-stun, meaning "sometimes they fight, like war, Indian fight."

Attracted by the advertisement, Mr. and Mrs. Abraham H. Cowherd, with their daughter Isabel and the Thomas Harkinson family, embarked on a launch from the foot of Denman Street in Vancouver, and camped for a weekend by the beach. The setting must have appealed to them because in the spring of 1910, Abraham Cowherd and Thomas Harkinson rented a launch and towed up a small barge loaded with lumber to build the wooden floor and walls of a tent base, plus essential supplies for the summer—an iron stove, lanterns, dishes and tools. Unfortunately, by the time they returned after school closed in June, everything was gone. They never did find out who had cleaned out their belongings, but suspected beachcombers. This problem continued to plague residents in years to come. Nevertheless, the families returned and built and became two of the first to stay at Brunswick Beach every summer.

The Cowherds and Harkinsons weren't alone on their piece of paradise. Many visitors, campers, and hikers heading for the Lions travelled to Brunswick Beach on the Terminal Steamship's *Britannia* and sternwheeler *Baramba*. A government dock, built around 1910, was convenient for about two years for unloading passengers, but finally collapsed from the heavy seas generated by the Squamish winds. After that, the ships would blow their whistles about halfway from Bowen, and Brunswick Beach campers and cottagers would quickly haul out their boats and row out to prepare for unloading passengers. These passengers were sometimes well soaked with sea water by the time they climbed down the ship's side on rope ladders and scrambled into the small boats.

Advertisements continued to attract potential property owners, some write-ups offering enticements that were not entirely accurate. In March 1912, the Vancouver *Province* announced under a Real Estate heading: "Brunswick Beach on Howe Sound beckons you. The route of the Peace River railway [sic] lies very close and at this point [sic] and there will undoubtedly be a station and so the beach will be more than ever accessible and more than ever the refuge of Vancouver people from the noise and dust of the constantly expanding city." By this time, prices ranged upwards from $150, with $10 cash down and $5 monthly payments.

In June 1914, *British Columbia Magazine* promoted Brunswick Beach as a "splendid site for the building of summer cottages and camping homes." The writer predicted that if the syndicate that held it in trust was to put it on the public market, it would become one of the most popular summer resorts on the Pacific coast.

Although it appeared to be an idyllic location, outside business, particularly logging, did encroach on the summer residents. A log flume carried timber down the hillside beside Magnesia Creek. Lumbermen used the Cowherd shack as an office in the family's absence, and built a large bunkhouse on two of the other lots. They logged some of the largest cedars on the surveyed land, but did finally agree to reimburse the lot owners $60 per tree.

During the late 1920s, a Mr. Norman built a hotel on the point of land between Alberta Bay and the original Brunswick Beach. It was a one-storey, wood frame building with encircling verandahs, the waves of Howe Sound washing the rocks on three sides just below it and a 360-degree view of mountains, islands and water. It should have been highly successful, but the Great Depression interfered and it appears that no one ever stayed there. By the mid 1930s it had been left to rot, and finally burned down.

More and more campers and summer residents stayed in cottages and tents beside the water. They did not have electricity until 1960, but a crude water system supplied their needs from early days. It consisted of a collection of hoses and galvanized and copper pipes that were wired together (clamps were expensive) and channelled water from a creek higher up the hill.

Norman's Lodge, on the point of land north of Alberta Bay at Brunswick Beach, c. 1928. The lodge was built just before the Great Depression, and apparently never did open for guests. It was later abandoned. *(BB)*

Just over 2 kilometres (1 1/2 miles) south, Saint Mark's Anglican Church of Vancouver set up a summer camp on Lions Beach during the 1920s. Blanche Loutet, who first visited Brunswick Beach in 1932, recalled that the young people used to row from the Beach to Saint Mark's camp once a week to buy ice cream cones and chocolate bars from the camp's launch. The launch sometimes brought a few Brunswick Beach fathers as passengers on weekends. More and more families purchased Beach property over the years, some as resales. By 1933 the Loutets, Edwards, Rhymes, Smiths, Elliots, Stainsbys and Ryans were established there.

When construction began during the 1950s on the Pacific Great Eastern Railway line and the highway between Horseshoe Bay and Squamish, the long-time residents must have watched with mixed feelings. But for those who were building permanent homes and cottages, the activity matched their excitement over their own building development, which was being made much easier because of rail and highway access. The railway line was laid parallel to the shore and the row of cottages, only about 300 metres (1000 feet) to the east of the properties. Railway and highway crews stayed in camps at Brunswick Beach, and an access road was cut up the hill to the highway. The roar of rock blasting and the clank and rumble of heavy machinery continued for some time. Monks Logging Company was operating above the highway, and its trucks followed the dusty road down across the tracks, then to the north behind the houses to its log-booming grounds at the end of the beach.

Gradually peace returned, with only the thunder of daily freight and passenger trains and the hum from the highway to break the stillness. Several residents built permanent homes and two early owners passed their properties on to their children. Noreen and Stan Copp took over his parents' lot in 1957, and their children have become third-generation Brunswick Beachers.

The adults enjoyed get-togethers and made the Sun Salmon Derby an annual family social event. The salmon weigh-in headquarters was at Sunset Marina, a few kilometres south, and usually the beach at Alberta Bay became crowded with fishermen and their families camping overnight to be sure of an early start. Some also used the Brunswick Beach properties as a parking lot.

In 1960, the long-awaited water and electricity systems were installed and the ritual of a bath in a tin tub in front of the fire was gone forever. Typical of the residents' community spirit, they banded together to install the water lines themselves, each family taking responsibility for planning one aspect of the construction. The electricity was an unexpected bonus. The developer of Lions Bay, Bob Nelson, could not sign up enough electrical power purchasers there to fulfill the criteria for his subdivision agreement. He approached the Brunswick Beachers to see if they could help him out by signing up for electrical power in their development. They were delighted, and his contract was saved.

Probably as part of their celebration, they held the first of many annual August barbecues. Each year they would set a theme—nursery rhymes, western village, South Pacific, etc.—and spend many hours planning and designing costumes and decorated sets. In 1974 the community arranged for the Royal Hudson steam locomotive to stop at the beach crossing. Residents dressed in outlaw and dancing girl costumes to entertain the tourists on board, providing each passenger with a small gift.

Today about 92 percent of the residents live there full time, but only four of the early families remain. Enthusiasm for the barbecues appears to have waned.

Bowyer Island

A few of the smaller Howe Sound islands have been privately owned, some since the 1890s. Pasley Island, a long finger of land at the entrance to the Strait of Georgia, was purchased by the Bell-Irving family in 1909. Later in the century they sold shares for individual lots to other families.

Southeast of Gambier and due north of Horseshoe Bay, Bowyer Island lies just offshore, settled in the water like the rounded shell of a giant green tortoise. In 1926, Herbert Bingham was looking for island property in Howe Sound. When he stopped on Bowyer for lunch, explored the forested land, then found a clear stream trickling over the rocks, he decided that he had found the ideal location for his family's summer home.

A strange bargeload headed to the island from Horseshoe Bay some time during the next year—eight goats, a cow, two horses and some crates of chickens. Other bargeloads brought lumber and several workmen, hired by Herbert to build a large, Spanish-style, white house with green trim for himself and his wife, Annie. They also built a barn, a home for the Binghams' son Carl and his family, and a caretaker's cottage. Annie Bingham called their land her "Treasure Island."

Bowyer Island, c. 1932. Herbert Bingham, who owned the island, built a 12-metre (40-foot) model lighthouse on the island's southern promontory. *(JA)*

The original home was a showplace. A large verandah encircled the house, and lush gardens bordered the beach, with flowers, vegetables and fruit trees—all barricaded from the foraging goats. Herbert Bingham imported a large generator so he not only had lights in the house, but also lamps on posts lighting the path down to the dock. He built an ornamental lighthouse on the south-facing peninsula, which they called Lighthouse Point. Annie, who was a meticulous housekeeper, also baked bread and stored her perishable supplies in an underground fruit cellar.

Carl's daughter, Justine Armstrong, remembers rowing across with her family from Horseshoe Bay in the 1930s. Later, a motorboat made travelling much easier. In 1995, Justine shared memories of her early days there: "The original goats multiplied dramatically, until they overran the island and ate all the underbrush. In those days [during the Great Depression] people were on Relief, and my grandfather had men up to shoot the goats. They shot a hundred of them. Finally there were just ten left, and we saw the same ten for years when we went around the island in our boat. Now we're overrun with deer and they're eating all the underbrush.

"In the 1920s and early 1930s," Justine recalled, "we had bonfires on the beach, huge ones. My brother Carl and I asked our friends to come and stay with us. We had a wonderful time. We'd take a day and hike all over the island. We found old bones of goats and we did a lot of fishing in those days, good fishing. Not anymore. One time we found a dead octopus. We thought it was a body in the water. We pulled it out and it had the longest arms. We did have fun.

Carl Bingham Jr., Herbert Bingham's teenaged grandson, with the body of an octopus he and his sister Justine found near the shore of Bowyer Island, c. 1935. When they first spotted it, they thought it was a drowned person. *(JA)*

"I remember a coppermine there. We would row over to the island's west side and, with a flashlight to light our way, walk on planks to the end of the tunnel. It was wet in there and very dark."

After Justine and Carl Jr. married, and each had families, they moved into their own places on the island. For a long time after their grandparents died, the family tried to maintain the original buildings, but finally decided that they couldn't keep them in repair. Justine explained: "Not long ago, we decided to burn the old places down. It was very exciting. We had a fireman up there, and a bunch of people, and the fireman went down below and lit a match in the big house, then later burnt the other places down. For all the years it took to build the places and look after them, it was all gone in half an hour."

The family has no regrets. They have all built new homes and developed a large playground and barbecue area where the big house used to be.

In the 1960s, Justine's father sold some of the land on the west side of the island to a group of 18 doctors and their families. They call their portion "Kildare." Other lots on the south side were later sold and became Bowyer Island Estates. The family still retains 10 hectares (25 acres) for their personal use. Justine's and Carl's children, and now their children, today spend many contented hours on their Treasure Island.

Passage Island

In a two-room driftwood cabin, Jack Thompson lived the lonely life of a hermit on Passage Island, with his black-and-white cat for company. He had lost his toes to frostbite when following the lure of gold in the Klondike, but could still climb the steps up to his home and beachcomb around the rocks. During the Great Depression, with no job and no money, he had decided to live off the land and built his home on the small, rocky island between Point Atkinson and Bowen Island. He lived in one narrow room furnished with a bunk, a stove and table. A small coal oil lamp provided light in the long, dark evenings. He used the tiny second room to store crates and boxes that had washed up along the shoreline. Fish, a vegetable garden and a small stream barely provided sustenance, but he was fortunate in having friends who would drop off clothing or food, or just tie up their boats and stop by for a cup of tea and a chat. His prized possession was a tattered flag that flew from the cliff above the cabin. During the period of his stay, his tiny home burned down twice. He rebuilt, but finally left the island in the late 1940s.

The British Columbia government had considered using the 13-hectare (32-acre) island as the site of a lighthouse around 1870, but they eventually built at Point Atkinson. Vancouver businessman J.C. Keith purchased the land in 1893 for $32, and it stayed in the Keith family until the death of Mary Isabella Keith. Her executors put it up for sale in 1959. The provincial government again decided against using the island, this time as a recreational site, because they felt that it was too small for development, and precipitous cliffs made the island too hazardous. The eventual buyer that year requested that neither his name nor the purchase price be released, although it appeared to be in excess of $7000.

Phil Matty, a realtor, purchased Passage Island in 1965 for $60,000. He had it subdivided into 62 waterfront lots, chose one for his family, and has lived there since 1971. In 1995, 23 homes graced the rocky shoreline, each specially designed to suit their location, with windows facing magnificent views of Vancouver, the Strait of Georgia and Howe Sound islands. The residents travel to and from the mainland in their own boats.

A secluded path winds through the woods, with smaller trails leading to the private homes. The trees are precious, and the residents are careful to preserve them as well as the slow rhythm of the Passage Island lifestyle.

Keats Island

As with the other picturesque islands on Howe Sound that began by attracting campers, then full-time residents, city folk who were looking for the sequestered life discovered Keats Island.

When Henry Brown moved there about 1905, he and his family enjoyed an isolated existence on land facing Gibson's Landing. He had bought his land from John Hooper, one of Keats' first settlers and the site's original owner. Loggers had recognized the value of the island's timber, and logging roads crisscrossed the otherwise undisturbed landscape.

Henry set to work to turn his acreage into a flourishing estate. He built a barn and a two-storey house with a front porch at the head of the small bay. Flowers, shrubs and vegetables enhanced the grounds around his home, and orchards produced prolifically. A group of labourers cleared the rocks from his land and used them to build low boundary walls. Evidence of these walls lasted for many years after the property was abandoned. The men used some of the rocks to dam a water reservoir at the top of a high bluff overlooking the estate.[2]

The Browns lived a quiet life, since few people lived on the island. Henry would often row across to Gibson's Landing in the evening to pick up his mail and catch up on local news.

The idyll came to an abrupt end in 1920 when fire engulfed their home. Mr. and Mrs. Brown moved away and left caretakers in charge of the land. Their daughter's family, the Scotts, often visited there during the summer, but after Mr. Brown died in 1921, his wife decided to sell. A portion of Keats Island's history came to an end, but a unique project replaced it.

In 1922, the Convention of Baptist Churches of British Columbia decided to establish a summer camp near Vancouver or Victoria. Early in 1926, the committee charged with locating appropriate land heard about the availability of the Browns' farm property and visited it. Very impressed with its potential, they deposited $200 and obtained an option to purchase at the selling price of $12,000. That summer they held their first camp, with primitive facilities, as a training course for Sunday School teachers. Although enthusiasm was high, the required capital was scarce until a group of Baptist businessmen formed Keats Island Summer Homes Ltd. later that year. Distributing shares for $25 each, they also sold leases for cottage lots to Baptist families. The families could build cabins on these lots, around what would later become the Keats Island Baptist Camp. The lease money would be used to finance the camp.

Keats Island residents meeting the Tymac ferry at the old wharf, c. 1948. Meeting the ferry on a Friday evening was one of the big social events of the week at Eastbourne on the northeastern shore of the island. Some of the Friday ferries were called "Daddy Boats" as so many fathers worked in Vancouver during the week and spent weekends on the islands. *(Pay)*

The 99-year leases began to sell for $200 to $350 in the spring of 1928. The leaseholders' agreements included stipulations that they would maintain an interest in the camp and would not use alcoholic beverages. If they decided to sell their leases, the company would have the right of first refusal. Only those who supported the religious aims of the camp would be allowed to purchase a lease. Although other families were attracted to the island's seclusion, those at the Baptist camp enjoyed, in addition, their Christian fellowship. By 1930, families occupied about 12 cottages on the outskirts of the camp. They were basic one-room buildings set on logs or rocks, with no insulation or ceilings.

The camp connection had practical advantages for the cottagers. The Union Steamship Company agreed to provide daily service to the wharf, and a camp store was available for basic necessities. The community was established on a financial practicality, but in future years its idealistic base was to cause problems.[3]

By the 1980s, the number of waterfront cottages surrounding Keats Island Baptist Camp continued to grow. The camp still held popular programs that attracted Baptist summer visitors, and the original purchasers remained firmly supportive. However, as new leaseholders took over, their relations with the camp became strained because of their lack of commitment to the original lease objectives.

In recent years, regulations have clarified the requirements for sale and transfer of leases, and the camp leaders have actively promoted cottager involvement, recognizing that the important relationship between the two groups must continue and flourish. Today the co-operation has forged a strong bond between camp and cottagers, allowing them to work together to develop projects such as a joint water-supply system that benefits all parties.

In 1996, Keats Camps celebrated its 70th anniversary of providing successful programs for campers. Many of the 70 cottages have passed down in Baptist families to children and grandchildren.

Keats Camps shares the island with two other groups. Eastbourne is a distinct community on the eastern shore made up of over 150 cottages. The residents don't have much contact with the camp.

On the north shore, at the Corkums' farm site, the Barnabas Family Ministries camp has added another Christian influence to the island since 1987. Howie Corkum, a Vancouver high school principal, purchased the farmland in the early 1930s. Unmarried, he encouraged his nephew Richard to visit from Nova Scotia in the summers to help out. When his uncle died in 1978, Richard inherited the farm, moved there and married. Homesick for the east coast, he sold a one-third interest in the land to the Barnabas Family Ministries group, which agreed to care-take it and use it as the site for their camps after he moved back to Nova Scotia. This group holds nondenominational conferences for adults, with the aim of strengthening the family.

The group renovated the old farmhouse, using it as a bed and break-fast for camp visitors, and built a new 12-room lodge overlooking the breathtaking views of Howe Sound and the mountains to the north. Surrounded on three sides by lush forest, it is an ideal location for peace-ful study and introspection.

Alta Lake

About the same time that the original Howe Sound and Northern rail line was in the planning stages, Alex Philip, a tall, good-looking man from the state of Maine, opened the Horseshoe Grill at Columbia and Hastings Streets in Vancouver. In 1910 he married his childhood sweetheart, Myrtle. One day the following year, a rough-looking character in a cow-boy hat and buckskin jacket sat alone, eating in the restaurant. He told Alex about the isolated cabin in which he lived beside the Pemberton Trail, close to lakes alive with trout eagerly waiting to jump at a hook. Alex's dream had always been to open a fishing lodge, so he and Myrtle arranged to visit the stranger, Mahogany John Millar, at his stopping house and explore the promising lakes.

The ferry *Bowena* delivered the pair to Newport. Harry Judd's stage took them to the Bracken Arms Roadhouse at Brackendale, and the next day they set out on horseback over the narrow trail beside the Cheakamus River, guiding their horses around boulders, down sharp inclines and over steep hills. When they finally reached Millar's cabin, they sampled his 50-cent meals and lodging. Fishing in Millar's Lake (now Alpha Lake) and Summit Lake (now Alta Lake) proved to be even more satisfying than they had expected, and with the beauty of the vir-gin forest surrounding them, they knew that they had found the land of their dreams.

They saved $700 and in 1913 bought four hectares (ten acres) from Charlie Chandler, a pre-emptor, on Alta Lake's northwest shore. The next year, while Alex stayed at the restaurant in Vancouver to build up essential

Myrtle and Alex Philip pausing along the Pemberton Trail, 1911. They were heading north on their first visit to Alta Lake. *(WMA)*

funds, Myrtle, her father and brother led horses packed with supplies up the Pemberton Trail to their lake. They cleared land and built a small sleeping cabin, then the two-storey main building from hand-cut and peeled logs. Many years later, Myrtle, a lively, white-haired 94-year-old, explained that they had called it Rainbow Lodge "because it was a dream we'd been chasing; it was our pot of gold. But it was the rainbow trout that brought us here."[4]

The PGE railroad came through at the opportune time for the Philips and brought not only their essential supplies and railway workers to feed, but also fishermen, hikers, trail riders and boaters on excursions from the city. For $2.50 return and 35 cents for tea, tourists could travel the PGE for an unforgettable wilderness trip. Word spread about the outdoor mecca and the delicious meals served at the Lodge.

Other guest house owners joined the Philips in attracting visitors. Russell Jordan's two-storey Alta Lake Hotel and store at Mons was successful until destroyed by a forest fire in 1930. South of Rainbow Lodge on the west side of Alta Lake at Harrop's Point, Bert and Agnes Harrop built cabins and a tea room in 1920. A coffee shop also served the railway workers. Its history was unusual. Russ Jordan, who had supplied the workers with refreshments at the Cheakamus camp, simply moved his building to Alta Lake when the construction moved north and continued business as usual.

Rainbow Lodge, Alta Lake, in the early 1900s. When Myrtle and Alex Philip built the lodge, it was a dream come true—they had always wanted to own a fishing lodge in the wilderness. It was also a great success from the start. Visitors came to Alta Lake every year on the Pacific Great Eastern Railway to fish, hike, sail and ski in an unspoiled wilderness. *(VPL 31672)*

The Philips opened a small store and Myrtle became the first postmaster at Alta Lake, a position she held for 33 years, from February 1915 until January 1948.

In 1925, the Union Steamship Company initiated "The Magical Day Sea-Trip on Howe Sound." The next year it became "Sea and Rail," Sunday excursions jointly sponsored by Union Steamships and the PGE to Brandywine Falls and Alta Lake.[5] The day-trippers travelled by ship to Squamish, by rail to and from Alta Lake, and then by ship back to Vancouver. The Philips hosted the eager tourists, serving tea and snacks. The Rainbow Lodge became so well known that in the 1940s, guests from as far away as Winnipeg came to ski, skate, trail ride, honeymoon and simply enjoy the out-of-doors.

The tiny Alta Lake community built its first school in 1931 for the ten to twelve resident school-age children. As might be expected, the community-minded Myrtle became a member of the first school board and later continued when Alta Lake amalgamated with the Howe Sound

District School Board in the 1940s. When the Whistler municipality built its new school in 1976, they named it for this energetic woman.[6]

The number of Alta Lake visitors increased yearly, attracted by the serenity and beauty, some camping near the lakes, some purchasing land for small cabins, but the lack of road access limited the numbers and kept the community secluded. In 1959, the Tyrol Ski Club was the first to take advantage of the ideal ski conditions on Whistler (formerly London) Mountain, the initial step in the eventual development of the multimillion-dollar Whistler ski resort.

Point Atkinson

At the opposite end of Sea to Sky Country, the Point Atkinson lighthouse continued to flash its signal at the entrance to Howe Sound, and the light-keepers dedicated their lives to its upkeep.

Walter Erwin, with his wife Rhoda's support, had tended the light for 30 years when he retired due to ill health in 1910. He received the Imperial Service Medal and a pension of $33 per month.

Thomas Grafton, an early settler on Bowen Island, had assisted Mr. Erwin for over 20 years and was appointed his successor. That same year, construction started on a hexagonal light tower, the one we still see today, and by 1912 a 55,000-candlepower light flashed far out over the Strait of Georgia. A small cabin housed a new fog alarm powered by internal combustion engines, air compressors and diaphones. The old steam engines ended their lives in the sea.

Walter Erwin and his wife would have enjoyed the sparkling new duplex with its long porch and lawn, much admired by the Graftons. By some oversight, the builder had forgotten to include a bathroom and had to convert the kitchen into a lavatory.

While the construction was underway, Tom maintained the 24-hour watch. Lightkeepers must keep daily records, and often he and Walter Erwin had mentioned the problem with a smoky haze from Point Grey, where logging operations spewed smoke into the atmosphere. Many times the lightkeeper had to start the fog alarm because of this overcast.

The handwritten log books, usually merely describing wind direction and weather, sometimes included entries detailing unexpected events. On December 27, 1912, Tom Grafton wrote: "Gasoline launch broke down drifting onto rocks on Point men calling for help Launched boat but before we could get to them the Launch struck the shore throwing the

Point Atkinson lighthouse, at the entrance to Howe Sound. In 1938, after Thomas Grafton was killed in a fishing accident, Ernie Dawe took over as lightkeeper. The hexagonal light tower we see today was built in 1912. *(VPL 16528)*

men in the water rescued the two men but could not do anything with Launch as the wind was very strong and a heavy sea put the Launch high and dry."

In spite of the new machinery, breakdowns still occurred at any time of the day or night. Though the lightkeeper had an assistant to look after the light while he slept, good men willing to work for low pay were hard to find. Tom Grafton endured a series of unreliable helpers.

His log described one such frustration on October 1, 1913: "11:10 PM light turning must have stopped some time after assistant was to have called me at midnight I woke up 1:05 AM found that light was stopped run up to tower started light revolving then looked for man found him asleep in fog alarm woke him up and told him that that would not do sleeping in his watch when he told me to go to hell and blackguarded me with foul talk I told him to get out of the fog alarm and as soon as it got daylight to leave the station he left 6:30 AM for Caulfeilds to catch boat for town."

During the Graftons' tenure the PGE North Shore railway lines were laid within walking distance of the previously isolated lighthouse, and trails connected the family to nearby homes. In many ways it was a good life, but one which ended sadly for Tom Grafton in 1933 when he was fishing from his boat with dynamite, which he commonly used to stun the fish that then floated to the surface. He died when the dynamite exploded in his hand. His family, friends and neighbours mourned his loss.

Despite tragedy, the light continued to send its warning beams across the water and signal the entrance to Sea to Sky Country.

CHAPTER 9

THE SEASONS OF RECREATION

The boon of days spent in Garibaldi Park is, we believe, to lift us a little higher above animal content, to rouse us to some divine impatience with dullness and inertia, to attune our hearts to hear this great land's challenge: "Give me men to match my mountains."

—Garibaldi Park brochure, British Columbia
Department of Lands, 1929

A trio of hikers, laden with backpacks, emerges from a dark hemlock forest into the bright sunshine. Behind and below them stretches a deep gorge, scoured out by glaciers thousands of years before. Jumping from rock to rock they cross a small river, the cold water milky with sediment from the melting glacier above. Blueberry bushes and wild flowers line the banks, and plump mushrooms merge with the forest litter.

The ground is softened by snow meltwater, and they climb more slowly in the thinner air. Passing the tree line, they reach the lip of a huge canyon stretching into the distance below them, more evidence of glacial action. The rocky slopes here are almost totally devoid of vegetation. They stop to rest, gazing in awe at magnificent, snow-capped Mount Garibaldi rising to one side. Ahead, a vast snow field shimmers in the sunshine. The hikers are minuscule and insignificant in the vastness of the desolate landscape.

Crossing a shallow valley, they slip and stumble over rocks—glacial till deposited by the receding glacier high above them. The sound of their laboured breathing and the whistles of the little furry marmots are gradually drowned out by the roar of water from a rushing creek—icy, clear water. They stop to fill their water bottles.

Reaching a mountain meadow, the hikers follow a trail knee-high in flowers—a palette of green, red, yellow, purple, pink and white. They stretch out under a deep blue sky, surrounded by a photographer's dream, hearing only the intermittent boom of boulders tumbling down a distant raging watercourse and a loud CRACK! from the glacier. Volcanic peaks and valleys spread out to the far distance, and a turquoise lake reflects the clouds overhead. The hikers boil water for tea on a small camp stove. For them, and countless others, a day in Garibaldi Park will be a lifelong memory.

Mountain Climbing

The old register from the Howe Sound Hotel on Bowen Island shows that Atwell King, George Martin and Arthur Dalton from Vancouver stayed overnight on August 10, 1903. Later, Mr. Dalton recalled the visit in an interview for the Vancouver Archives with Major J.S. Matthews: "We were on our way to make the first ascent of the western Lion [mountain]. Captain Cates, of the Howe Sound steamer, put us off at Hood Point, and we had to make arrangements with the hotel keeper to sail us across the sound to the eastern shore opposite, so that we could commence our

The Lions. These beautiful peaks have been a favourite hiking and climbing area since the late 1800s, when climbers travelled to Lions Beach by boat and set off from there. *(UBC BC1250)*

ascent of the western Lion. It looks all very simple and pleasant here on this hotel register, but as a matter of fact we had quite an argument with the hotel keeper before we could persuade him to sail us across the sound."

The Lions were the highest of several mountains on Howe Sound. A Squamish legend named them The Sisters or The Twins. Early Vancouver men, pioneering in a settlement with very few women, fantasized the two peaks as Sheba's Breasts or Sheba's Paps. However, the most common image conveyed was of the heads of two lions, and a British survey chart showed Lions Gate or First Narrows as the entrance to Burrard Inlet's inner harbour around 1891.

When the climbers arrived at a small beach below The Lions on the east side of Howe Sound (near what is now Lions Bay), they began their climb. After two days of scaling treacherous cliffs and pushing through thick undergrowth, roped together for safety, they reached the western peak. They stood, overawed by the magnificent views north up Howe Sound and as far south and west as Vancouver Island and the Fraser River delta.

Although these men assumed they were the first white men to ascend the western Lion, a contradictory report from July 1889 claimed that honour for H.O. Bell-Irving. With Chief Joe Capilano and some Squamish men on a hunting trip, he paddled to a beach below The Lions, camped overnight, and left early in the morning for a rugged climb. Mr. Bell-Irving said that, following a herd of wild goats, they reached the peak of the western Lion, but did not leave a record of their achievement. He also described his climb to Major Matthews: "The party then camped on 'the back of the Lion.' In the early evening Chief Joe wished to display the prowess of one of his Indian companions. He asked me to take out my watch and time the lad, who, stripped naked, raced up the rocks to the peak, where he waved to those below, and returned within the remarkable time of approximately 20 minutes."

Because the party did not leave any sign of their presence at the top, they had no proof other than their word that they, in fact, were the first white people to climb the western Lion.

At least three other parties scaled the eastern and western Lions in 1903, and during the next few years many climbers, including women, attempted the ascent, most crossing the Capilano watershed (which was itself becoming a popular recreational area) from the south to reach the mountain. The men wore hob-nailed boots, puttees (a long strip of cloth wound spirally round their legs from ankle to knee) to protect their legs from branches, and old, well-patched clothing. The ladies wore hats, long skirts, long-sleeved blouses with high necks, and heavy nailed boots that peeked out from under their long skirts. They had their problems in remaining ladylike. Frank Smith described their appearance as "hideous" in his reminiscences, published in 1958 in *The Mountaineer* magazine: "Of course the skirts had to be discarded at the first opportunity, bringing into view a pair of bloomers which ballooned out from the waist and draped over the knees. A more unsuitable garment for brush could hardly be conceived. It simply invited every snag to grab it, with some disastrous results. On the return trip, the cached skirt was resumed for the business of crossing on the ferry and reaching home [Vancouver]. Woe betide the young lady who, through some accident or failure to locate the cache, found herself skirtless. A rule of the Ferry Company forbade any lady to board the boat in bloomers and on one occasion an unfortunate bloomer girl had to send word across and have some relative come over with a skirt to enable her to get home."

The climbers devised their own version of packsacks for carrying supplies. They wrapped a large sheet of oilcloth around their hiking essentials and strapped the bundle to their backs with army surplus packstraps. To retrieve any article, they had to unroll the whole bundle.

Hikers and mountaineers were discovering new challenges, sailors spent Sunday afternoons within the sound's boundaries, and campers and picnickers enjoyed the natural shorelines. By the turn of the century, the discovery of the area's recreational potential was well underway.

Garibaldi Provincial Park

The mountainous 195,000 hectares (480,000 acres) of Garibaldi Provincial Park stretch from just north of Squamish to beyond Whistler. The park's namesake, Mount Garibaldi, is an extinct volcano and was named after Giuseppe Garibaldi, a famous Italian patriot. The mountain's traditional Squamish name was Chy-kai, meaning "mountain of the dirty snow," because the snowfields are covered with dust blown from the lava beds and cinder cones. The park area is, in fact, part of a volcanic belt, the Pacific Ring of Fire, which stretches from Japan, north to Alaska and south to South America.

Glaciers, lakes, rivers and mountains have attracted hikers and

The first cabin built at Garibaldi Lake by Jim Spilsbury's Queen Charlotte Airlines Ltd., 1948. The company built several cabins in the area during the late 1940s and early 1950s to house summer and winter visitors. This one had electric lights and a radiotelephone. *(UBC/Spils)*

climbers since the early 1900s. In 1902, when the first climbers explored Mount Garibaldi's lower slopes, they hiked in from Squamish and found glaciers that have since receded by at least 2.5 kilometres (1 ½ miles). In the summer of 1907, three separate groups of intrepid climbers made the first ascents of Mount Garibaldi. The Vancouver Mountaineering Club, later the BC Mountaineering Club, held regular camps in the alpine meadows high above the Squamish Valley. Over the years the members climbed several peaks, naming them and other notable geographical features, some after outstanding climbers.

Lakes and rivers were also being named. Between Daisy and Alta Lakes, Brandywine Falls was an impressive cascade that later became a popular tourist viewpoint. It received its unusual name from a pair of railway surveyors in 1910. Bob Mollison and Jack Nelson were impressed by the 62-metre (200-foot) waterfall, and a friendly argument ensued about its height. Each man believed that his own estimate was correct, so Mollison bet his bottle of wine against Nelson's bottle of brandy. A length of survey chain confirmed that Mollison had made the closest estimate, and very likely a celebration ensued beside "Brandywine Falls."

Pristine Garibaldi Lake has long been a favourite camping area,

A Queen Charlotte Airlines seaplane, c. 1950. The company used these aircraft to bring guests and surveyors to Garibaldi Lake. At 1460 metres (4790 feet) above sea level, the lake was free of ice by mid-July. *(UBC/Spils)*

hidden high up behind The Barrier, the lava wall at the top of Rubble Creek. In 1919, climbers launched a small boat, the *Alpine Beauty*, on the clear waters. Three years later, Mountaineering Club members had another boat built in Vancouver and transported it in pieces, by horseback and backpack, up to the lake where they reassembled it.

Vancouver florists and garden shop owners heard about the lush alpine meadows bursting with blooms of many rare plants that grew in the rich volcanic soil. Some arranged to have pack trains bring out loads of plants destined for Vancouver gardens. Botanists and geologists were also attracted to the unique, easily accessible landscape. Mainly due to pressure from the mountaineering clubs, the BC government protected the area by naming it a Park Reserve in 1920. In 1926, the Garibaldi Park Act established it as a provincial park. Later, during the 1960s, the southern area was sectioned off and renamed Golden Ears Provincial Park.

As the construction of the Pacific Great Eastern Railway made previously unexplored areas more accessible, a few lodges were built to provide climbers with a place to stay before and after their ascents. Alpine, Garibaldi, Lake Lucille and Daisy Lake Lodges, all near the park boundary,

Ad published in a British Columbia Department of Lands pamphlet, 1929.

offered accommodation, meals, boats and pack horses, with good fishing nearby.

Over the years, mountaineering club members, trappers and prospectors marked trails and cleared paths through many of the passes and up into the mountains. The park was developing a reputation that attracted climbers from many parts of Canada and the United States and had earned it the name "St. Moritz of North America."

The first lodge within the park, Garibaldi Chalet, opened in the winter of 1946 at the foot of Mount Garibaldi. Two Norwegians, Emil and Ottar Brandvold, and Ottar's future wife, Joan Mathews, selected a site beside the Elfin Lakes near Diamond Head and built a two-storey log chalet that could house 30 guests. After clearing an 11-kilometre (7-mile) trail from the park border, which they used to pack in necessary building material, they cut carefully selected logs, and draft horses dragged them to the site. A traditional sod roof topped the lodge.

Garibaldi Chalet was famous not only for holding the record as the highest west coast lodge, at an elevation of 1800 metres (5900 feet), and for being the first private ski lodge in British Columbia, but also for Millie Crowell, the cook, and her delicious meals, especially her wild blueberry pies.

For 25 years the Brandvolds welcomed outdoors enthusiasts, and they, themselves, continued to explore the land they loved. When they finally gave up their lease early in the 1970s, a part of Garibaldi Park's history came to an end. The chalet still stands, unused, and an article in the fall 1992 issue of *Heritage BC Newsletter* suggested it could be demolished if the BC government decides the structure has become a hazard to public safety.

Garibaldi Park is the scene of summer and winter activities, becoming more popular every year with visitors from all over the world.

Whistler Resort

Bands, banners and motorized floats accompanied over 500 skiers, skaters, hockey players and curlers in a torchlight parade along Vancouver's downtown streets. It was February 1961, and while banners flew from Georgia Street lamp standards, radio, television, newspapers and billboards exhorted people to support Vancouver's bid for the 1968 Winter Olympics at Whistler Mountain in Garibaldi Park.

In 1960, a group of Vancouver businessmen formed a committee to search for a site suitable to host the Olympic games. They looked at mountains accessible to Vancouver, studying snowfall, wind patterns, hydro availability and road access. Garibaldi Park's fantastic skiing potential attracted their interest, and they formed the Garibaldi Olympic Development Association (GODA) to spearhead their project. Helicopter surveys confirmed that Whistler Mountain would be the ideal location, offering the potential of a variety of slopes and trails, appropriate elevations, and a climate not subject to extreme cold or to Chinook winds that would melt the snow. The fact that ski slope development had not yet started, and that Whistler had no electricity, water or road access, did not deter them, nor did the estimated development cost of $10,080,000.

Great disappointment followed the Canadian Olympic Association's selection of Banff as the site Canada would put forward to the International Olympic Committee. Whistler was a close second. GODA held out hope for hosting future Olympics, and the government later optimistically reserved 21.5 hectares (53 acres) as a future Olympic village site.

In 1960, the same year that GODA became prominent, a Norwegian, Franz Wilhelmsen, enthusiastically persuaded a group of his friends to form the Garibaldi Lift Company. They did studies of the skiing potential and developed plans for the necessary ski lifts on Whistler Mountain. They needed an expert to analyze the terrain for ski slope development and suitability, and hired the well-known Austrian Willy Schaeffler. His 1962 report was so encouraging that the company began to make serious plans.

Government leases for the Crown land came more easily than the development capital of $800,000, but by the summer of 1965, crews were hard at work felling trees for the lift lines and ski runs, assembling the gondolas and T-bars, and constructing the first buildings. The provincial government developed a much-needed, rough, gravel road between Squamish and Whistler at the company's urging. The Garibaldi Lift Company celebrated on January 1, 1966, by hosting a banquet and free trip up the mountain for the Alta Lake residents, who probably were watching all of this activity with mixed reactions. The official opening was February 15, 1966, and even the most optimistic of the developers would not have predicted the ultimate success of their project.

Whistler Ski School started in 1968 and encouraged novice skiers to try the slopes. Helicopters had been used for the mountain's surveys, to

Whistler Mountain's first gondola, at what is now Whistler Creekside, completed in 1966. The "Gondola" building in the background was called the Gondola Barn. By the mid-1970s, skier lineups wound around the parking lot. *(WMA 89.940 WMSC)*

pour concrete for the tower bases, and as standby emergency service. But in 1966 they were used for the first time in Canada for heli-skiing on otherwise inaccessible slopes and glaciers, where the quality of powder skiing attracted the most experienced skiers. Today, heli-skiing with well-trained guides is a popular business for several Whistler companies. They must follow strict government safety regulations never considered in the 1960s.

Over the next few years, Garibaldi Lift Company added new facilities and by 1974, 5000 skiers per day were using them. The Roundhouse, originally a day lodge, then a ski shop and cafeteria, provided warm-up facilities at the 1800-metre (5900-foot) level, high above the bustle of the village. Skiers could ski down one of several runs from there or take a lift to a higher run. Summer skiing on the glaciers and cross-country skiing became popular, and the number of visitors increased, but accommodation and essential services in the valley barely provided supply equal to the demand.

By 1997 the lifts on Whistler Mountain could transport 23,495 skiers (or snowboarders) per hour and over a hundred marked runs criss-crossed each of the two mountains (Whistler and Blackcomb). Whistler Village, at the foot of Blackcomb Mountain, opened in 1980 on the site that the government had held in reserve for an Olympic village. By 1997 the Blackcomb lifts could carry over 29,112 skiers per hour. The snow-making capacity on Blackcomb can cover 146 hectares (360 acres), 9 percent of the total skiable terrain. On Whistler, snowmaking capacity covers only 64 hectares (158 acres), about 4 percent of the skiable terrain.

The Whistler/Blackcomb ski area is considered one of the best in the world. It recorded over 1.74 million skier visits in the 1996–1997 winter season, believed to be the highest number of skier visits for any resort in North America. This is exactly what the Garibaldi Olympic Development Committee had predicted to the Olympic organizers back in 1961.

Rock Climbing

Within sight of Mount Garibaldi, the Stawamus Chief rises solidly to 670 metres (2200 feet) above Squamish. The second largest freestanding granite monolith in the world (Gibraltar is the largest), it borders the east side of the highway south of the town. The Chief is one of the more well-known granite climbing areas in North America and is popular both for its accessibility and for the high-quality, glacier-scoured granite. Early visitors to the area thought a shape high on the main cliff resembled an Indian's face in profile, and so the Chief received its name.

The first recorded climb took place in 1957 at the South Gully, then known as Goose Rock. With the completion of the highway from Horseshoe Bay, more and more rock climbers discovered the challenging cliffs and gullies during the 1960s. The year of the "Great Leap Upward," 1961, Jim Baldwin from Prince Rupert and Ed Cooper from Seattle were the first to climb the face of the Grand Wall. Every night they would come down and camp at the base. After the media discovered them, curious observers often lined the highway. Assistance for the impoverished climbers poured in—a hotel room, clothing, food and even extra pitons from the local blacksmith. The men inserted a total of 136 bolts in the rock for belaying ropes. Over one month later, they reached the summit. The route they established became very popular with climbers who followed.

A novice ice climber using crampons and ice axes to practise on a glacier-scarred rock in Murrin Park, south of Squamish, 1996. During some winters, nearby Shannon Falls freezes like a giant icicle and attracts climbers to its potentially dangerous face. *(DA)*

Over the years, climbers have opened up nearly 300 routes on the Chief and the surrounding granite cliffs. One of the climbs is considered the most difficult in Canada. The Little Smoke Bluffs, just north of the Chief, is a popular rock face for beginners; on most weekends throughout the year, travellers on the highway can pick out tiny figures on the grey rock. Many other granite cliffs north of Squamish attract hundreds of climbers. Free climbs, without ropes or pitons, have become very popular. The climbers use only their hands and feet, encased in rubber shoes, wedging them in cracks and around edges—a real adventure climb.

The Federation of Mountain Clubs of British Columbia has developed and maintained the trails on the Chief and the Little Smoke Bluffs, and in 1987 purchased some of the most well-used land there to protect it from commercial enterprise. The Federation has been promoting the area as a future provincial park.

Another challenge, more unusual than rock climbing, is the frozen face of Shannon Falls just south of Squamish. The falls are 335 metres (1100 feet) high and are among the highest in the world. Every few years the weather is cold enough to turn the waterfall into a collection of giant icicles hanging from the mountainside. During the period of the big freeze, the ice becomes a mecca for some local rock climbers. With steel crampons attached to their boots, they climb the lower section with ice axes, then drive ice screws into the surface to hold their climbing ropes to reach the top, never sure when the ice will detach from the rock face. The ice can begin to crack apart very quickly when the weather warms, and climbers have to be cautious that a melt has not started. Surprisingly, it is not rated as a very difficult climb, but is considered rather as a rite of passage for rock climbers.

Sports Country

Perhaps the area should be renamed "Super Sports Country," as the terrain lends itself to such a variety of opportunities for novice and experienced outdoors enthusiasts. Many mountainsides are ideal as take-off points for hang-gliders. Rapids in the Green and Squamish Rivers attract whitewater adventure rafters. Hiking trails echo not only to the clump of hiking boots, but also to the crunch of mountain bike tires. Recently, mountain bike associations have helped design and build biking trails around Alice Lake and Paradise Valley near Brackendale, and in the Diamond Head area in Garibaldi Park. A 150-kilometre (93-mile) Sea to Sky Mountain Bike Trail is planned between Squamish and D'Arcy, north of Pemberton. It is the only project like it in the world. "Heli-biking" is also popular for those wanting to reach more isolated areas by helicopter.

Howe Sound waters off the Squamish Spit are considered the best in Canada for windsurfing. Since the early 1980s, windsurfers have congregated there to "catch the wind" that can push the boards up to 60 kilometres (37 miles) an hour. The Squamish Windsurfing Society considers the location an advanced windsurfer's park, but some of Whistler's five lakes are good spots for beginners.

Seven provincial parks from Squamish north to Whistler offer facilities for hiking, camping, canoeing and fishing. Rainbow, cutthroat and brook trout and Dolly Varden rise to lures in dozens of glacier-fed streams and rivers. Between Britannia and Whistler, about 23 lakes are easily accessible and provide good fishing.

While most of the recreational attractions are found in the heights, another group of outdoor enthusiasts enjoys the depths of the waters of Howe Sound. Divers first began to explore the sea life there during the 1950s, often without scuba tanks, attracted by the area's accessibility to Vancouver and the numerous beaches lining the eastern shore from

Scuba divers at the marine park, Porteau Cove, 1997. This is a rich spot for divers, as the sunken hulls of several ships attract a variety of sea life. The white buoys in the background mark an underwater trail of tires cabled together between the hulls. *(DA)*

which they could enter the water. Because of housing developments along the waterfront, divers' access by land has become limited. Many now use the marine parks at Porteau Cove—25 kilometres (16 miles) north of Horseshoe Bay—and at Whytecliff in West Vancouver. Whytecliff was the first underwater marine park registered in Canada in which no marine life may be removed from within its boundaries.

Barbara and George Brooks once ran a diving store in North Vancouver and now run their own business making wetsuits. They have been diving since the early 1970s and consider Howe Sound good, but not excellent, for experienced scuba divers. Prime factors that attract divers are prolific marine life and good visibility. Silty water from the many creeks and rivers flows into the Sound at the same time as the plankton blooms in summer, sometimes reducing visibility to 1.5 to 3 metres (5 to 10 feet). In winter though, especially near Whytecliff Park, visibility of over 30 metres (100 feet) reveals an underwater world of octopus, wolf eels, salmon, ling cod and, at deeper levels, sponges that cluster on rocky cliffs. George recalled one dive where he was surrounded by thousands of small herring, enclosing him in a moving mass of fish that maintained a certain distance from his body.

At Porteau Cove, five large ships were sunk to form an artificial reef in hopes of attracting more marine life to the sandy bottom. This has been a popular place for training divers.

Fast-moving water carries nutrients to feed marine life, but Howe Sound doesn't have many narrow passes that will force the water to surge. To find prolific sea life in the area, many divers travel by boat to favourite spots in the sound, like the eastern shore of Anvil Island where the water moves more quickly and visibility is good.

They never know what they will find underwater. Off Bowyer Island at "Toilet Bowl Reef," it is rumoured that an octopus makes its home in an old, discarded toilet bowl.

Camps

Howe Sound's scenic beauty and outdoor opportunities have had a profound influence on the lives of thousands of children. Early in the twentieth century, the concept of Christian camps developed to promote children's religious education as well as encouraging healthful living. The

Keats Camps on Keats Island, 1994. The camp offers comfortable sleeping cabins and a dining tent. On the waterfront, off the photograph to the left, campers enjoy kayaking, swimming, windsurfing, sailing and canoeing. *(KC)*

Camp Artaban dock with "the Beach House" in the background, c. 1941. The house, designed as a guest house about 1916 by Vancouver businessman and dairy farmer Robert P. McLennan, is part of the camp and a Gambier Island heritage building. *(Camp Artaban collection)*

Young Men's Christian Association (YMCA) was the first to establish a camp on Howe Sound's shores, in 1907, when the YMCA Boy's Camp, later Camp Elphinstone, opened on the west side of Howe Sound with about 35 boys. It was the first of its kind in British Columbia. More than 80 years later, girls were allowed to attend.

By 1926, the boys from Camp Elphinstone were able to perfect their water skills by sailing or canoeing to visit four new church camps operating nearby—Camp Artaban Anglican camp on Gambier Island's Long Bay, Camp Fircom United Church camp at Halkett Point on Gambier, the Salvation Army Camp Sunrise near Langdale on west Howe Sound, and the Keats Island Baptist Camp. St. Mark's Anglican Church Camp also opened in the early 1920s on Lions Beach below what is now Lions Bay. Later, other camps operated on Anvil and Bowen Islands and at isolated Potlatch Creek. Howe Sound's close proximity to the city was a great advantage.

Although campers paid fees, many children from inner city homes were able to attend for a minimal or subsidized charge. The outdoor experiences, combined with an emphasis on Christian living, helped shape the future lives of many campers, some of whom returned later as counsellors and leaders. Recollections of camp ceremonies, singing around the campfire, outdoor chapel services, hiking, boating, swimming and other outdoor sports activities left the campers with lifelong happy memories and encouraged many to continue exploration of the great outdoors.

CHAPTER 10

THE SERIES OF CHANGES

*Urban sprawl is spilling up from Vancouver, along the curvy
Highway 99, just as years ago it headed east into the Fraser Valley.
Population pressure and Canada's highest land values are bringing
new money and new perspectives on land use to old mill towns like
Squamish, turning the Sea to Sky corridor into the north arm of the
Lower Mainland octopus.*

—Doug Ward, "Squamish: The suburbs move
north" in the Vancouver *Sun*, August 5, 1995

T he watchers stood silently under the overcast sky, their binoculars trained on the trees along the river bank. The stench of rotting fish permeated the air, and the rushing water eddied along the shore, lapping at hundreds of fish carcasses. Over 200 eagles, their wings spread to dry, perched in the cottonwoods lining the bend of the Squamish River, taking respite from their feast.

Every winter, along a 50-kilometre (31-mile) stretch of the Squamish River that runs near the neighbourhood of Brackendale, approximately one-third of North America's bald eagle population returns to feast on spawning chum salmon. Birdwatchers counted 37,000 eagles during a one-day period in 1994. That many birds could eat about 1.8 tonnes (2 tons) of fish daily during a good salmon run if waters are low enough not to wash the fish bodies downstream.

The residents of the Squamish community are justly proud of their unique visitors and hosted their eleventh annual Brackendale Winter Eagle Festival in January 1997, attracting birdwatchers from great distances. Concerns about logging close to the eagles' habitat led to the establishment of a 600-hectare (1482-acre) provincial reserve at

The lower Squamish River and estuary. Howe Sound is at top; Squamish is at top right. Log booms ready to be towed to the mills can be seen all along the river. *(UBC/MB BC1930/492 10899)*

Brackendale in October 1996 and another 10,000-hectare (24,700-acre) area in the Tantalus mountain range farther north of Squamish. The reserves protect the tall conifers that the eagles need for roosting and perching, but the eagles themselves are not protected. In 1995, the Nature Conservancy announced that it planned a $3 million campaign of research, salmon enhancement, public education and compensation for private landowners. The Forest Alliance of BC donated $2 million to the campaign.

Squamish

During the early years of the century, business in Newport (Squamish) had begun to boom, just as the Howe Sound and Northern Railway promoters had predicted. In 1912, two hotels, Armstrong & McCallum's General Store, McKinnon's Restaurant and a sawmill provided facilities and employment for the growing population. The developers continued to upgrade the streets, adding wooden sidewalks (which sometimes washed away in the yearly floods), and connected a water system, gravity fed by the Stawamus River. In a reflection of the general enthusiasm for the town's future, Vancouver's *News-Advertiser* predicted on October 20, 1912, that "this town of Newport bids fair to be one of the wonder towns of the West."

It never did quite reach the heights predicted. In 1914, the Squamish Incorporation Act optimistically provided for the community's incorporation as a city, although it did not even have a local government. Thirty-four years later, Squamish officially became a village with village commissioners.

In 1920, numerous businesses lined the main streets of "downtown"

Squamish, that area that abutted Howe Sound. Newport sawmills as well as the Walsh & Day Lumber Company sawmill provided ready lumber for building. The residents no longer had to ship lumber from Vancouver or use logs to build their homes.

Daily, steamships tied up to a long wharf that was large enough for ocean-going ships. Electricity brought welcome changes in lifestyle to many of the population of 500. The PGE company used water from the Stawamus River, just north of the granite monolith known as Stawamus Chief, to generate power for their facility as well as the more densely populated areas of Squamish. Electricity flowed only until midnight at first. BC Electric began providing power in 1949.

Harry Judd's 16-year-old stage business continued to offer mail and passenger service. Business must have been prosperous, as Harry and W. James, proprietor of the Cheakamus Hotel located at the Cheakamus railway station north of Squamish, took out a half-page advertisement in the 1920 British Columbia Directory:

FISHING ON THE CHEAKAMUS!
Leave Vancouver on Terminal Steamship boat
from the foot of Carrall Street to Squamish.
Fare $2.00 return

At Squamish wharf take mail stage run by
H. JUDD OF BRACHENDALE [sic]
up the Squamish Valley 10 miles to the
CHEAKAMUS HOTEL. Fare $1.50 return

From the Cheakamus Hotel, rate $2.50 per day,
excellent fishing is secured in the Cheakamus
River, in Alice Lake and Bhrom [sic] Lake.

This space is subscribed to by the undersigned,
who offer an excellent outing at minimum
charge.

H. Judd, Auto Stage	Cheakamus Hotel
Brackendale PO	W. James, Prop

Of the men registered as Squamish residents in the 1920 British Columbia Directory, approximately three-quarters were PGE employees, and as the railway construction finished in the Squamish area in the 1920s, the need for workers on the line diminished. A certain number of employees stayed on to run the railroad maintenance shop, but many more moved on to other locations. Some businesses closed down and property values nose-dived. Squamish again became a quiet country town.

Brackendale and the upper Squamish and Cheakamus Valleys remained mainly agricultural land. Although most of Brackendale's population of 200 was living on farms, Bradney's Road House, Hugh Mills' boarding house and Whitaker's general store and post office provided services for residents and visitors.

The natural beauty and lush farmlands continued to attract newcomers. The rivers, an element that made the valley so appealing, were also the source of continuing frustration. Although residents expected yearly floods from the Squamish, Cheekye and Mamquam Rivers, some floods severely damaged homes and farms. The 1921 rains that devastated Britannia also washed out parts of Squamish and Brackendale, as well as the railway lines. In 1933, flood waters again reached record levels.

On October 19, 1940, however, heavy rains raised the rivers' level to

The Squamish Hotel, previously the King George Hotel. In the early 1900s, the hotel provided accommodation for tourists, loggers and railway workers. *(SPL 14.2)*

Squamish's main street, Cleveland Avenue, during the 1921 flood. The man in the photograph is walking on the floating wooden sidewalk. *(SPL 6.74)*

such an extent that, combined with a 4-metre (13-foot) tide, they produced the worst flood in Squamish's history. As the waters poured over the dykes erected around the town's perimeter, the roads became roaring rivers and water submerged properties to unprecedented depths. Near the railway workshops, the flooding rose to within half a metre of some houses' ceilings. Residents with two-storey homes leaned out of their upper windows to watch as men in rowboats rescued people from low-lying areas. Children claimed chunks of the wooden sidewalks and poled their way through the floating debris—firewood, apples, pumpkins, oil drums and even bridges. Water in the stores reached counter level, farm stock and chickens drowned and tons of hay were ruined. Railway lines washed out, and telephone and telegraph communications broke down.

The dykes, instead of preventing the flood, were, in fact, containing the water and raising its level. Drastic measures were necessary and sections of the dykes had to be dynamited. The water roared out through the holes and gradually the level lowered.

The next day the water was less than knee deep, but it had left its

Cleveland Avenue during the 1940 flood. *(SPL 4.23)*

slimy, stinking residue. Mud caked every surface that the water had touched—mattresses, furniture, walls, and floors that warped and heaved, leaving linoleum buckled and cracked.

One flood victim wrote his memories of that day for the Squamish *Times*: "Got bread at MacKenzies [store] hanging through an upper window. Walking hither and thither on floating sidewalk, saw Mr. Hale waist deep in water in the house with the family floating on the sidewalk."

The flooding problem still wasn't resolved by the 1950s. In 1947, engineer Fred Feeney was commissioned by the provincial government to study the flooding and make recommendations to prevent further devastation. Although his comprehensive report made sound suggestions for flood control, there was no money from the government to pay for construction of major dykes until Squamish and the surrounding communities incorporated as a District Municipality in 1964 and brought their combined pressure to bear on the BC government.

A series of dykes was built in the early 1970s and partially solved the problem, but even this was not sufficient to prevent further inundation, as high river and tidal waters could flow in behind the dykes. Two major floods, in 1980 and 1981, precipitated the community's firm resolve to complete the system of dykes. They did so in 1984 with the assistance of a $3 million grant from the provincial government and $1 million contributed by Squamish. A large flood gate was constructed at the mouth of the Squamish River. It could be closed to hold back the salt water at very high tide levels. Squamish's floods, a consistent part of the town's history, were no more.

Another influx that affected Squamish, this time in a positive manner, was the increase of industries in and around the town. Logging had always been the main source of employment, but now a sawmill, the F.M.C. chemical plant (built in 1965) that produced chlorine and caustic soda for the pulp industry, a railcar manufacturing plant started in 1974, and a major deep-sea docking facility for pulp and lumber shipments all added to the town's income. The economy was improving steadily.

Probably the most influential influx to the municipality was people. By the time a road opened between Britannia Beach and Squamish, the mine had slowed production and many Britannia residents moved north to the town, some even transporting their houses with them. Similarly, families from the Woodfibre Pulpmill townsite made the move across Howe Sound to locate in an area from which they could drive to Vancouver and also enjoy a much more extensive social life. By 1981, Squamish municipality had a population of 10,000 people, and thousands more were driving through every weekend on their way to Whistler.

Perhaps the greatest impact came when Squamish was discovered by Vancouver residents looking for lower priced housing. Between 1981 and 1995, the population rose by 4000. About 2000 people per day were commuting to Vancouver along Highway 99, willing to accept the minimum 90-minute round trip in exchange for affordable homes. Some people working in Whistler found relief from the high-priced land there and commuted daily north from Squamish. Although Squamish house prices were rising, based on the increased demand, it was still a much cheaper place to live.

Some long-time Squamish residents are concerned that the area will lose its identity as a slow-paced logging town. Logging companies operating near Squamish have had to deal with opposition from some of the newer residents, without long-term ties to the industry, who are strongly in favour of preserving natural habitat. Squamish's image was destined for change in the 1990s with the addition of several major fast-food outlets and malls along the highway. The debate continues among Squamish residents: are they seeing progress or a step backwards?

A MacMillan Bloedel logging crew yarding and loading logs in the mountains north of Squamish, c. 1955. Logging has been the main industry in Squamish since the late 1880s. *(UBC/MB BC1930/338-342)*

Gibson's Landing

In the early 1900s, the two villages on Howe Sound's shores experienced opposite levels of economy. While the railway swelled Squamish's population and provided jobs, the men of Gibson's Landing did not have the opportunity to work for a large local business. LePage's Glue Company had built a large factory in 1898 to process glue from dogfish, but it closed down after a short time. Wages came mainly from road building, logging and fishing. Many families farmed.

A few residents were entrepreneurs and attempted to develop their own small businesses—a charcoal operation, milk delivery, cartage and taxi services. William W. Winn bought J.S. Chaster's store in 1912 and developed it into a profitable venture under the name Winn and Son, General Merchants. They sold bread and fruit, boots and dry goods, gasoline and engine supplies, and feed for farm stock, and also rented out boats. Later they offered delivery service in a Model T Ford truck. Emma Fletcher also operated a store and post office, and L.S. Jackson, brother of George Jackson, an early Vancouver butcher, opened a meat market for a few years.

George Hopkins bought land in 1907 at what is now Hopkins Landing, just northeast of Gibson's Landing. He and his sons began construction of a tug boat, the SS *Hopkins*, in 1909. They later used it in a profitable towing business and also built two large scows, which they would charter out.

Mr. Hopkins subdivided his land into smaller lots, as did F.C. Grantham who established Grantham's Landing just south of Hopkins. Grantham built some summer cottages and called his resort "Howe Sound Beach," which became popular with summer visitors. He also set up a real estate office at the entrance to School Road, but business was slow if not nonexistent.

And so the quiet community's commercial efforts were small and often unsuccessful—until the Stoltz Shingle Bolt Company began development on Mount Elphinstone late in 1919. A sound enterprise, it provided employment for two years for many of the local men. Bunkhouses, a cookhouse, a stable and a blacksmith's shop supported the large crew. In the 1930s, the company's logging operations near the Squamish River provided employment opportunities there also.

The business that probably provided the most financial assistance to the community was the Howe Sound Co-operative Canning Association. The land around Gibson's Landing had always produced prolific quantities of berries—strawberries, loganberries, blackberries—as well as plums, and a group of residents decided to take advantage of the crop. They built a cannery in 1922 near Payne Creek. The company paid local growers four cents a pound for their berries during the first year of operation, and proudly retailed their jars of "Four Square" jam. The high quality of the product won the British Empire Trophy the first year.

Later, the W.H. Malkin Company of Vancouver acted as distributor, and the jam was sold under the label "Malkin's Best." The company's production expanded and additional help was required. Women and girls were able to earn 40 cents an hour in 1924, adding to their family income. By 1931, increased berry yield forced double shifts for a period of time because the ripe fruit would spoil if left overnight.

Motor cars were scarce, so farmers used any available means—including bicycles, wheelbarrows and goat carts—to transport their fruit to the cannery. Production was high and shipments left regularly for Vancouver. Distributed from there, Gibson's Landing jam could be purchased in many parts of the province.

Unfenced, free-ranging cows enjoying Armour's Beach just north of Gibson's Landing, 1935. The town's first Municipal Hall was later built here. H. McCall photo. *(EPM)*

A major blow to the small company came when improper processing resulted in moldy and spoiled jam. Retailers angrily reported that lids had blown off some of the cans. It was essential to retool the factory with a new steam-cooking process, but money was scarce during these Depression years and the cannery's financial problems worsened as the general economy improved during the Second World War. Fruit growers no longer needed the extra income from the cannery, and employees demanded higher wages as other jobs were now available. The reduced co-operative membership finally voted to cease production in 1952.

Thus the business that provided solid financial assistance to the community throughout its leanest years and drew the people together in a shared enterprise came to an end when jobs in logging, sawmills, the Port Mellon pulpmill, fishing and small business became available for Gibson's Landing residents.

The next big change came in 1967 when, overnight, the residents of Gibson's Landing found themselves living in a new village. The results of a referendum held on December 9, 1967, approved the change of name to "Gibsons," 80 years after the founder, George Gibson, filed for his pre-emption. Some people objected to giving up the original name, as evidenced by the 106 "No" votes, but the 320 "Yes" votes prevailed.

The village lifestyle was slow-paced, the economy depressed, and the population less than 2000 when, in 1971, a new project moved into the still-isolated community. The Canadian Broadcasting Corporation (CBC) decided to stage its new family television series, *The Beachcombers*, in and around Gibsons. It would show the adventures of ordinary people on and beside the sea. The unspoiled natural beauty of the setting, ideal weather conditions for the purpose of the show, and the willing co-operation of the Gibsons residents all added up to a perfect choice for a filming location.

At the head of the main wharf, the central stage for the production was a vacant liquor store, which soon became "Molly's Reach" restaurant. Much of the series' action took place there, and actress Rae Brown, as Molly, welcomed the cast. The stage setting, with its candy- and trinket-covered counter, coffee urn, tables and chairs, was so realistic that tourists frequently stopped in to try to buy lunch. Bruno Gerussi, a well-known Canadian actor, played one of the lead roles, and an 18-year-old Sechelt Band member, Pat John, held the key role of the young man, Jesse. The series, which started out with plans for a one-year season of 13 episodes, extended to two years and was so popular that the final episode aired 19 years later.

Four-pound cans of jam produced by the Howe Sound Co-operative Canning Association, c. 1935. To help create opportunities for employment in Gibson's Landing, some area residents got together to develop the canning enterprise, which for several years produced jam from the area's abundant berries and other fruits. *(EPM 935)*

Gibsons residents couldn't help but become involved in the spring and fall production schedules. The directors welcomed local schoolchildren on visits to the set. The cast and crew joined the annual Gibsons Sea Cavalcade, filming the actual activities, lighting up the wharf for the Friday night dance, and contributing to the fireworks display. They even produced one episode based on the day's events. For other shows they needed assistance in locating such unusual props as a 1930-vintage Model A Ford car and a pigsty. They advertised for rental accommodations for their cast and crew, and hired a workboat owned by a local resident. It became the *Persephone*, well remembered by committed viewers.

The series injected income into Gibsons' economy. Many local people were hired for walk-on roles, crowd scenes or as bit players. The directors used some businesses as filming locations, changing the signs to suit the script and recompensing the owners for lost revenue. They would also reimburse affected businesses when they had to close a street for a day. Local caterers, gardeners, carpenters and painters became part of the crew.

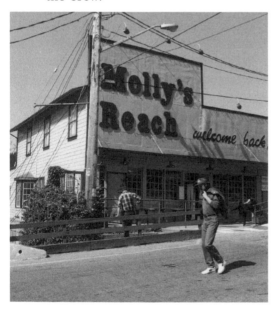

Molly's Reach, at the Gibsons waterfront, 1997. The building served as a furniture store and a liquor store before becoming the restaurant featured in the popular CBC-TV series *The Beachcombers* from 1971 to 1991. It is now open for business as a real restaurant. (*DA*)

People from Gibsons were generally pleased with the international fame the show brought to their town and enjoyed watching the show, as much for seeing their neighbours and local landmarks on the screen as for their appreciation of the stories. There were times, however, when the filming caused problems, for example, when the main street was closed while scenes were being shot. All noise had to stop, including radios, loud voices and car motors. That meant traffic came to a standstill, which was a real concern for people trying to reach the ferry docks or appointments by a specific time. Some motorists used the simple expedient of honking their horns if

CBC crew filming the popular television series *The Beachcombers* off the shore of Keats Island, c. 1975. Filmed in the Gibsons area, the series lasted from 1971 to 1991, 370 shows. *(EPM 1785)*

the wait was too long, which meant that the entire scene had to be reshot because of the inappropriate sound. In the meantime, the traffic could move on.

This memorable era in Gibsons' history passed when the CBC announced that episode 370 at the end of the 1990-1991 series would be the last. The size of the audience, 1.85 million viewers in 1980, had dropped to under 1 million, and attempts to increase the ratings had failed.

The calls of "Camera, sound, roll 'em" came back to Gibsons late in 1992, when a Los Angeles company spent two months filming the sinister Stephen King movie *Needful Things*, a far cry from the relaxed and family-oriented *Beachcombers*.

In 1983, Gibsons became a town, with a population of about 2500. Since then it has acquired a large marina and several new businesses, but still appreciates its history and unbeatable spectacular setting.

The Cheakamus Dam

From the 1950s, construction in the area north of Howe Sound increased yearly as the railway from Vancouver encouraged tourists, settlers and businesses to move inland, away from the shoreline. One of the first

The Cheakamus Dam under construction, c. 1956. One of the few earth dams in the world, this one had supporting walls built up with rock and gravel from nearby Rubble Creek. The Cheakamus River can be seen at lower centre. (*Gerry Chaster photo*)

major undertakings was BC Electric's construction of the Cheakamus Dam on the south shore of Daisy Lake, 37 kilometres (23 miles) north of Squamish. This project included construction of a tunnel to carry the water westward to a generating station on the Squamish River.

Engineers had studied the Cheakamus and Squamish Rivers and the surrounding lakes for several years as potential sources of hydro-electric development. In the 1920s, the city of Vancouver had even considered generating its own power from those water sources. In February 1955, the BC Electric Company (now BC Hydro) began construction on the $25 million project.

The workers lived at a specially built campsite on Cloudburst Mountain, near the PGE's Garibaldi Station. From that base, the crews went daily to the dam site and the tunnelling operation. Gerry Chaster was 29 years old in 1956 when he worked seven days a week, 6 p.m. to 6 a.m., as soil inspector on the dam construction. He recalled that debris from the bottom of The Barrier rockslide provided material for the earth-filled dam. The rocks and gravel had to be graded by size, deposited at the appropriate levels to achieve maximum stability and strength to hold back the water, then compacted in layers. The machinery ran 24 hours every day.

Drilling platform and crew working on rock drilling for the Cheakamus Power Project, 1955. The workers removed more than 294,000 cubic metres (over a million cubic feet) of rock to form the tunnel. *(BCH)*

Gerry remembers the unspoiled beauty of the forested land at Daisy Lake, with summer cottages between the shoreline and the PGE railway tracks. After the power company purchased the property that would be flooded by the reservoir, the cottagers simply left the buildings and contents in place, probably because it was too difficult to move their belongings. Gerry used to wander through the deserted homes, examining their contents—shelves of old books, bowl and pitcher sets, cast iron kitchen

Cheakamus Dam at the south end of Daisy Lake, just east of Highway 99, 1970. The dam, completed in 1957, is 27 metres (90 feet) high and 620 metres (2034 feet) wide. The dammed water flooded over 400 hectares (1000 acres), forming the storage basin for the Cheakamus Power Project. *(BCH)*

stoves, brass bedsteads covered with mattresses and blankets. Later the buildings were burned to the ground.

The storage dam on Daisy Lake's south shore is the only section of the development that is evident to travellers passing along Highway 99. During the dam's construction between 1955 and 1957, nearly 350,000 cubic metres (457,800 cubic yards) of rock and earth were built up across the Cheakamus River to form a dam 27 metres (90 feet) high and 620 metres (2034 feet) wide. Where previously some swamp and the cottages had surrounded Daisy Lake, dammed-up water flooded over 400 hectares (1000 acres) to form the project's storage basin.

Other crews worked on the tunnel, four metres (thirteen feet) wide, that would carry water from the depths of the lake westward, under Cloudburst Mountain, to penstocks on the Squamish River. One crew worked from the eastern end of the tunnel, near the Cheakamus River, while another crew drilled through solid rock from the Squamish River at the western end.

Bill Flett was working for Mannix Construction, the company in charge of constructing the section of tunnel leading to the Squamish River, in the summer of 1955. He was responsible for concreting the inside of the tunnel walls where the steel and timber shoring supported unstable rock. He and the other workmen lived in a two-storey bunkhouse near the eastern end of the tunnel. Good meals at the cookhouse and double sleeping rooms made life comfortable.

To reach his work site, Bill took an electric "man car" through the tunnel. The air was foul. Echoes bounced off the walls when no work was in progress, or the harsh sound of air drills reverberated from wall to wall. A line of electric lights strung along one side of the roof provided shadowy illumination in the darkness. At some spots, water poured through cracks in the rock, soaking anyone passing beneath. The volcanic rock formations were filled with glacial sediments and debris and, in places, allowed water to pass through freely.

When the men had free time, they enjoyed fishing in the nearby lakes or visiting the pub at the nearby Garibaldi Lodge (which could be quite a wild place according to some). Occasionally they would go on a jaunt to Vancouver. This entailed either taking the PGE train or walking eight kilometres (five miles) south along the tracks to the end of the road from Squamish and taking the only taxi to the dock, where they boarded the steamer *Bonnabelle* to Vancouver. On the way back they could catch the train at Squamish and get off at Garibaldi Station or again walk the tracks.

The tunnelling operation took about two years. In 1957, an official party waited quietly about 1000 metres (3281 feet) underground to watch the final breakthrough between the two tunnels. Proudly, the workers drilled through the thin layer of connecting rock. The two segments of the 11-kilometre (6 3/4-mile) tunnel were within centimetres of a perfect meeting. The men had used 782,500 kilograms (1,725,000 pounds) of dynamite and removed 294,000 cubic metres (384,537 cubic yards) of rock.

The power development was one of only a few in the world to use two separate, parallel-flowing rivers. The tunnel diverts most of the southerly flow of the Cheakamus River, which runs through Daisy Lake, and carries the water 11 kilometres (6 3/4 miles) to a point 270 metres (885 feet) above the Squamish River to the west. From there, two huge penstocks, made of steel 7 centimetres (2 3/4 inches) thick, carry the rushing water down to the six-storey-high generating station on the river's shore.

Used primarily as a "peaking" station to fill the requirements at "peak" or high-demand power periods, the electricity that is generated flows 19 kilometres (12 miles) south to Cheekye on power lines that then join the main lines coming south from the Bridge River plant.[1]

Highway 99

The Squamish Highway, which winds along the base of the Cascade Mountains above Howe Sound from Horseshoe Bay to Squamish, was originally called the Seaview Highway. It has also been labelled everything from one of the great scenic highways of the world to British Columbia's Killer Highway, infamous for its rockfalls, floods, debris torrents and car accidents.

Men who were unemployed during the Great Depression were the first to work on the road. In 1931, the government paid labourers ten cents an hour to work with pick and shovel widening the trail north from Britannia. They reached Browning Lake (now part of Murrin Provincial Park) before giving up. It was almost a road from nowhere to nowhere, but at least the residents of Britannia found it useful for going on picnics. A few years later, BC Electric opened it as far as Squamish, but it was a narrow, rough track.

Squamish residents petitioned for a road to the city for many years, as their only access was by boat. Action began in 1949 when Gerry Chaster, who later worked on the Cheakamus Power Project, experienced the adventure of surveying the virtually inaccessible cliff faces between Horseshoe Bay and Britannia for the future railway line and highway. He recalled in 1997:

I started in January 1949 at Horseshoe Bay. We [the surveying crew] boarded at various places. I was at Mrs. Lamb's and most of the others were at Ericsons'. Mrs. Ericson was the crew cook. She knew I wouldn't eat onions so she made me an onion pie!

We were transported by a 25-foot [7.6-metre] powerboat to the designated work site, bailed off the bow of the boat onto the rocks, and clambered up the cliffs with our lunches and survey equipment—axes, transits, levels, level rods, etc. On occasion, the boat operator made several runs to get each of us off—Howe Sound can be pretty ugly at times.

First day on the job the snow was up to my armpits. Around some of the rock bluffs we used two ropes—one to walk on and the other to hold onto. Exciting! Especially in freezing conditions. Near noon we would check to make sure none of us had fallen off a cliff. One day, just before quitting time, that happened and a fellow had a lung puncture and shock before we got him back to Horseshoe Bay and finally to the North Vancouver hospital.

On several occasions we had fellows from around the world on the crew. One Aussie came out on the boat and sat there until we had bailed off. Then he said we were all crazy and went back to town.

Our crew later moved to Porteau [Cove], where we used the old abandoned Deeks McBride gravel pit crew cottages as accommodation, cookhouse and eating areas. No running water and only outhouses. The owner of the site had donkeys that came to the cook each morning for a feed of hotcakes. In the winter we were sometimes isolated for weeks as the Squamish winds made it impossible to travel Howe Sound in any craft.

Because of the extent of the rockslides and the problems involved in cutting through them, we all wondered why anyone would ever think of putting a railway or highway through there.

Early in 1955, the same year the Cheakamus Power Project began, the first rock was dynamited to begin the $10 million, 37-kilometre (23-mile) highway project from Horseshoe Bay to Britannia. The contractor had to blast most of the road out of solid rock—in many places, vertical cliff faces. An estimated 8,200,000,000 kilograms (18 billion pounds) of rock were removed. Workers had to move all of this rock over the newly constructed railway line below, paralleling the road, so that they could dump it into Howe Sound. The engineers considered it the most difficult project they had ever undertaken.

After three-and-a-half years of construction there was a concentrated effort to surface the road to make it passable for August 7, 1958, the official opening, to mark Squamish's centennial celebrations. A 13-kilometre (8-mile) improvement to the stretch from Britannia to Squamish, worth an additional $50,000, began about a month before the opening. A preliminary rough blacktopping covered about half of the route from Horseshoe Bay on August 7, when a cavalcade of around 3000 cars, headed by Premier W.A.C. Bennett and Highways Minister Phil Gaglardi, left

West Vancouver and drove north on the 8-metre-wide (26-foot), winding, bumpy road. A speed of 40 to 55 kilometres (25 to 34 miles) per hour was considered safe. From Britannia to Squamish the rough, 4.5-metre-wide (15-foot) road took very steady hands on the steering wheel. At one point the road ran between a steep rock cliff on one side and a drop of 30 metres (100 feet) on the other side to the railway tracks below, with no guard rails.

A Vancouver *Sun* reporter, who described the ride as if it were a roller coaster, gave his impressions of the highway on September 4, 1958, almost one month after it opened:

Right now there are more bumps than benefits for unwary motorists hoping for a scenic outing along the 28-mile [45-kilometre] trip from Horseshoe Bay to Squamish. The road actually is in worse shape now than it was August 7 . . . Signs advertising periodic week-day closures posted at Horseshoe Bay give no indication of the shambles motorists must endure to get through to Squamish.

Sightseeing motorists are advised to limit their trips to the first 8 miles of view-point dotted smooth road that lures them on to Lions Bay.

The familiar "Sorry for the Inconvenience" sign is an introductory understatement of the year when applied to the next 7-mile [11-kilometre] stretch between Lions Bay and Porteau.

Hurriedly smoothed over with temporary paving for the highway opening a month ago, it is now a chewed-up, potholed section under reconstruction. At several spots construction activities squeeze traffic into hazardous one-way only lanes. [Between Britannia and Squamish] the rough, sparsely-gravelled surface is a mixture of potholes and washboard . . . the grader couldn't budge boulders sticking up through the road surface and couldn't collect enough gravel or dirt to fill in the holes.

Although drivers still complain about driving the Squamish highway today, the trip is more comfortable now than it was on the original road. Overly cautious drivers moving too slowly, or impatient speeders passing other cars on dangerous stretches, have caused hundreds of accidents that make many travellers cautious about using the highway, despite its unsurpassed views. But perhaps the most frightening events are those involving natural disasters. Since the highway opened, 13 debris torrents and 13 floods have roared down 13 of the 26 creeks between Horseshoe Bay and Britannia Beach, destroying nine highway and railway bridges and five culverts. Extremely heavy rainfall that swells the mountain creeks, the collapse of fill used to construct logging roads, and washed-out culverts have often triggered debris torrents.

The worst accident related to a bridge washout occurred on the night of October 28, 1981, when water and rock knocked out the middle span of M Creek bridge north of Lions Bay. Several vehicles plunged 15 metres (49 feet) into the maelstrom below, and 9 people were killed. In 1980 there were 8 deaths on the highway, but in 1979 there had been 14 fatalities, 274 injuries and 800 accidents. The government has replaced the original creosoted timber bridges with steel and concrete structures and is widening and straightening some sections.

Periodically, an alternate route through the watershed area from North Vancouver to Squamish is promoted, but the government consistently turns it down due to possible damage to the source of Vancouver's water supply.

The Horseshoe Bay to Squamish section of Highway 99 was barely completed when continuing pressure from Pemberton residents, joined

Clearing a rock slide on Highway 99, January 1960. Slides like this one are a continuing problem on the mountainous road. Charles Jennings/*Province* photo. *(VPL 45468)*

by the Whistler Mountain Lift Company and skiers, forced the provincial government to begin an extension north from Squamish. Although the construction was a little easier, the section through the Cheakamus Canyon called for rock blasting and hairpin curves. The road followed portions of the tortuous old pack train route and the hydro service road. Some bridges were merely two planks across a gully, and the road was so rough it rattled and threatened to shake apart any cars attempting to drive it, even at a snail's pace. The snowplow would clear the road on Saturday mornings only, which dictated the times that skiers could reach the hills. If two drivers met on the single track road, both would have to stop and shovel an opening into the roadside snowdrift before they could pass. Sometimes the drive took five hours from Vancouver, or longer, compared to today's one-and-a-half hours. Without suitable tires, cars would get stuck in the mud or snow, and the line-up would stretch out behind them. If it took too long, the motorists would drive back to Squamish and spend the night there before trying again. You had to be passionate about skiing.

Horseshoe Bay

West Vancouver council meetings were the forum for heated debates during the late winter and spring of 1951, and Horseshoe Bay was the topic. Residents were alarmed over plans to construct the first car ferry wharf on Horseshoe Bay's shoreline. Sea Bus Lines Ltd. had been operating a foot-passenger ferry between Horseshoe Bay and Gibson's Landing for several years, but the American-owned Black Ball Ferries had now applied for expropriation rights of the land so that it could construct a landing for car ferry service to replace Sea Bus Lines.

The West Vancouver reeve condemned expropriation as "a ruthless method, second only to the sword," and Horseshoe Bay residents predicted that a ferry landing would mean the end of the popular park and summer resort. Although the government refused the ferry company the power of expropriation, feelings against the change still ran high. One councillor predicted that the ferry would never be an asset and that policemen would be required to control the traffic. Dan Sewell, of Sewell's Marina and Landing, supported the Horseshoe Bay Community Association's opposition and told council that he had counted 140 fishing boats in the bay a Sunday earlier. He predicted boating disasters if a large ferry had to find its way through the small boats.

The Sea Bus Lines Ltd. vessel *Sea Bus* leaving Gibson's Landing for Keats Island, c. 1947. The company provided passenger service from Gibson's Landing to Howe Sound islands and the mainland before Black Ball Ferries began its car ferry service. *(EPM 834)*

Other sites had been studied, including Batchelor Bay, just south of Whytecliff Park, but Horseshoe Bay appeared to be the most practical location from an engineering viewpoint. The BC government approved a foreshore lease for the ferry company in May 1951, and the West Vancouver council added its grudging agreement, much to the relief of Sunshine Coast residents who were ardently supporting the ferry.

On August 11, 1951, MV *Quillayute*, flying the Black Ball flag, a black circle on a red field, initiated the route across Howe Sound to Gibson's Landing. It could carry 48 cars and 600 passengers, had a lunch counter, and made five round trips daily. Each round trip took 90 minutes. Predictably, some Horseshoe Bay residents were bitter about the ferry traffic noise and the large number of parked cars on the community's roads. The ferry service was there to stay, however; in September, council approved plans for Black Ball's construction of a two-storey building on the wharf to house offices for staff, a ticket office and waiting room. The wharf and offices were located at what is the western side of the present terminal.

Gradually, Horseshoe Bay residents and businesses settled into the routine of ferry whistles and traffic noise, but in less than two years the upheaval began again when Black Ball announced plans to initiate a Horseshoe Bay to Nanaimo service. When the reeve did not strongly oppose this proposal, the Lions Gate *Times* reported on page one, February 5, 1953: "Bay Association to Fight Black Ball. 'Appauled' with Reeve Ray's Stand—Horseshoe Bay Residents Adamant in Stand Against Augmented Black Ball Ferry Service to Nanaimo." The Horseshoe Bay Community Association once more sent briefs to the government and delegations to the West Vancouver council meetings in attempts to pre-serve the bay's park and oppose additional ferry service, which would mean more waterfront taken over for wharves, and heavier traffic both in Horseshoe Bay and travelling along narrow, winding Marine Drive. The residents reiterated their concerns about small boat safety, especially since the existing Gibson's Landing ferries actually turned within the bay's confines.

Once again, the residents' pressure was unsuccessful in preventing the new ferry service, but probably had a bearing on the West Vancouver council's decision to save parkland. Only one month later, on March 12, the District of West Vancouver announced that it would hold a public vote on two bylaws. One would authorize it to sell .33 hectares (.82 acres) of the Horseshoe Bay park for $80,000 to the Black Ball Line. The other would authorize the district to purchase, with $75,000 of the pro-ceeds, 16 hectares (40 acres) of land with buildings at Whytecliff Park and Whyte Island from Union Steamships Company Ltd. The people of West Vancouver supported this proposal.

Less than a month after the vote, wharves were under construction. The ferry, to be named the *Kahloke*, had already been in the process of a $1 million renovation for several months. In June 1953, Black Ball pur-chased the Heasman's Wharf property, a local landmark on the east side of the bay, and by August it was available for car-parking space.

The mountains echoed to the MV *Kahloke*'s departing whistle at 9:30 a.m., June 27, 1953, as she began her inaugural run to Nanaimo on Vancouver Island. She could carry 100 cars and 1000 passengers, and opened up wider vistas for travellers.

Earlier that month, a group of Horseshoe Bay residents sent a reso-lution to the Governor-General-in-Council, urging the government to refuse permission for a car ferry service until the Upper Levels Highway

The busy Horseshoe Bay ferry terminal, c. 1990. Ferries come and go to Nanaimo, Bowen Island and the Sunshine Coast. *(BCF)*

was built and could take the traffic away from Marine Drive. The West Vancouver *News* reported a few days later that the residents' spokesman said: "We have done our best, everything humanly possible, and now we can only wait for, and accept, the final decision." In the autumn of 1954, a second ferry, the *Chinook II*, expanded the service.

On June 17, one year later, West Vancouver announced the opening of their new park at Whytecliff. Cliff House offered a dining room and lanai, supper dances, a coffee shop and catering service.

In 1961 the British Columbia Ferry Corporation purchased the Black Ball fleet, painted the ferries blue and white, and added them to BC's Dogwood Fleet. Over the years, additional ferries improved services from Horseshoe Bay to Nanaimo, the Sunshine Coast, and Bowen Island. The fleet has expanded, not only in number, but also in the size of ferries.

In 1973 the BC government announced plans to remove the Nanaimo ferry terminal. The West Vancouver *Citizen* announced this surprising response on February 7, 1973: "Horseshoe Bay Faction Opposed to Removal of Nanaimo Terminal—Government Moves Despite Petition." Some of the merchants were appreciating the increase in business from tourists. Other citizens were vocal in their support of the removal of the ferries from the bay. Cooler heads prevailed, however, and service to Nanaimo continued.

The construction of the Upper Levels Highway across West Vancouver during the 1970s eased car access problems, but the increasing size of summer line-ups for ferries is, perhaps, an omen of the need for future expansion.

Gambier Island Copper Mine

Gambier Island residents rallied in 1979 to counteract the gravest threat in the island's history. A mineral company disclosed its plans to mine 252 million tonnes (280 million tons) of copper-molybdenum. The company built roads and camps and began exploration drilling, announcing that the project would involve the construction of several dams, a large tailings pond and huge rock storage piles. The operation would encompass two-thirds of the island's area.

Gambier Island's two trustees on the Islands Trust, Elspeth J. Armstrong and Beverly Baxter, led the battle to prevent the company from planning a giant open pit mine on the secluded island. The Trust was created by an act of the provincial legislature in 1974, with a mandate to preserve and protect the unique environment of the islands in Howe Sound and the Strait of Georgia. It was given some of the same powers as a regional district or municipality and was required to prepare community plans and enact land-use bylaws. Local trustees, elected for three-year terms, are members of the Islands Trust Council, along with elected trustees from the 13 islands that make up the Trust area. The Islands Trust committee members usually deal only with subdivision and zoning bylaws, and the possibility of a large open pit mine was one of the most serious threats they had faced to the future of one of their environmentally fragile islands.

The Trustees disclosed that the proposed Gambier Island project could result in an open pit of up to 2.8 by 1.2 kilometres (1 3/4 by 3/4 miles), over 300 metres (984 feet) deep. The 91,000 tonnes (100,000 tons) of rock blasted daily would end up in mineral and rock piles covering massive areas. Round-the-clock machinery operation would require floodlighting by night and would produce a continual dust cloud day and night. Ship loading, storage, transportation and hydro facilities would all have to be built.

The company claimed, rightly, that mineral exploration was permitted on Crown land under the Mineral Act. The 1974 Islands Trust Act, however, explicitly outlawed actual mining, and the 1979 Gambier Island Zoning Bylaw limited land use to recreational, residential and forestry.

For five years, individuals and committees petitioned government officials by telephone, letter and personal visits. Attempted legal interventions resulted only in frustration, but served to emphasize that more pressure had to be put on the government if citizens concerned about the environment wanted to see controls established over the use of Crown land.

The public outrage was so widespread and vociferous that the mining company decided not to continue with its plans. Pressure from the Gambier Island Preservation Society finally resulted in the provincial government's establishing a mineral reserve on the entire island in 1985. No future mineral claims could be issued.

One major battle was won, but residents still have concerns about larger developments and Department of Highways road standards. The department gives the final approval for subdivisions in the province and applies its own highway standards for any new subdivision on a Trust island. These province-wide standards are often in conflict with the standards islanders would like to see in their rural setting.

The peaceful and unique island lifestyle and ecosystem will only be maintained through the vigilance and continued involvement of those who live there and those visitors who go to enjoy what the island has to offer.

Water Ecology

Environmentalists have also been concerned with the threat to wildlife and fishery resources from logging and water pollution in Sea to Sky Country. Reforestation now usually follows logging, but many of the mountainsides bear the scars of thousands of denuded hectares that will remain for years to come, and the old forest habitats for some wildlife species are endangered.[2]

The waterways have borne more than their share of pollution. Howe Sound is 42 kilometres (26 miles) long and widens at one point to 35 kilometres (21 3/4 miles), with a depth of up to 325 metres (1066 feet). The Squamish River drains 90 percent of the 4000 square kilometres (1544 square miles) of watershed, which has been adversely affected over the years by the impact of coastal and island communities, two large pulpmills, a chemical plant, a highway, rail lines, mining, logging, a ferry terminal and a large port facility at Squamish. The District of Squamish discharges sewage from two treatment plants into the Squamish River and estuary. Even though the community of Whistler has developed a Liquid Waste Management Plan, people are concerned that the effluent could cause undesirable algae growth in the Cheakamus and Squamish Rivers, thus affecting fish habitat. The Cheakamus River is considered to be one of the most important suburban wilderness environments outside of the Lower Mainland, and the Cheakamus Dam has changed the river's physical and chemical characteristics.

For years the sound has been a thriving log booming area. This industry covered 947 hectares (2340 acres) of foreshore equalling 40 percent of the shoreline. As a result, rotted logs and debris cover large segments of the ocean floor. This type of bottom cover lowers the dissolved oxygen level and can result in the production of hydrogen sulphide. Only a limited number of aquatic species can survive in this environment.

In the past, the pulpmills discharged chemical effluent and dumped wood waste into the water, reducing or eliminating surrounding sea life. The whole food chain can eventually be affected as diving ducks and cormorants consume the contaminated fish and shellfish. Although the Britannia Mine has been closed for many years, the mine tailings previously dumped into the sound, and acidic mine drainage that still flows down the mountain, have discouraged the development of bottom-feeding undersea organic life. Dredged sediment from Burrard Inlet, which has included lead from paint on the hulls of ships at anchor in the Inlet, was, on occasion, dumped into Howe Sound. Seventeen salmon and trout spawning streams flow into this fragile ecosystem, which supports 80 kilometres (50 miles) of spawning grounds, almost all of them in the Squamish–Stawamus River system. Chinook, steelhead, pink, coho and chum salmon migrate from the Pacific Ocean to these rivers to lay their eggs from spring to late November.

In 1969 the federal government closed Howe Sound to commercial salmon fishing, but the waters are still popular for sports fishing, except in the northern section. The damage to the Squamish River estuary caused by overfishing, landfills, dredging, log storage and flooding has severely reduced the salmon stocks and eliminated the formerly prolific herring spawn in that location. Pulpmill effluents and mercury contamination from a chemical plant (no longer operating) severely affected shellfish, leading to commercial harvesting closures in upper Howe Sound in 1970.

In 1988 the federal government began testing for a particularly toxic group of chemicals—dioxins and furans—in aquatic organisms near British Columbia pulpmills. As suspected, high levels of these chemicals showed up in Howe Sound's prawns, shrimp and crabs. The Department of Fisheries and Oceans banned their harvesting in affected areas around the Port Mellon and Woodfibre pulpmills, and around Keats Island. By 1989 the Sound was closed to commercial crab fishing. Oysters around Gambier Island's shores contain unacceptable levels of zinc and copper, likely from the ongoing Britannia mine discharge.

And what have the people done to overcome these threats to the sea life in Howe Sound? In 1972, ten research stations around the Sound monitored pollution and recorded large pollutant discharges. The federal and provincial governments presented a proposed Squamish Estuary Management Plan in 1982. It has since been implemented.

Fisheries and Oceans Canada team at work in Howe Sound, 1997. The men are examining the effects on fish habitat of the acidic and metal-laden discharges from the abandoned Britannia Mine. Bruce Nidle, Project Research Biologist, rinses collected plankton into a preservative. Dale Marsden, a UBC graduate student, has just used an epibenthic sled to skim off invertebrates from immediately above the bottom sediments. *(DA)*

Bruce Nidle, Fisheries and Oceans Canada, collecting water samples near Britannia for future analysis in the laboratory, 1997. *(DA)*

Recommendations included the need for an environmental review process, including a review of development plans with public involvement. An area designation system set up a conservation designation on the west side of the estuary, industrial and commercial designation on the east side, and a planning and assessment designation in the middle area of the estuary.[3]

Since 1990, government agencies have monitored mill effluent dispersion, studying contaminants and water quality and analyzing bottom-feeding invertebrates. Some studies have shown increased liver lesions and distortions, and stunted growth of gill parts of fish near pulpmills, although contaminants in the flesh are lower than in the livers, which is important for fish consumption. The pulpmills' managers have been working to improve their production processes so hazardous wastes are eliminated, and they continue to participate in ongoing research. Pulpmills in Howe Sound, along with other coastal mills, are now required to conduct environmental effects monitoring programs and annual surveys of dioxins and furans.

In 1991, a three-day Howe Sound Watershed Environmental Workshop attracted professionals including marine biologists, oceanographers, environmentalists, geologists and representatives from Howe Sound's two pulpmills for a focus on available research, which was subsequently shared at public meetings.

The Murray A. Newman Field Station for Howe Sound Research is

The Murray A. Newman Field Station for Howe Sound Research on Popham Island, 1989. This privately owned nature refuge has been overseen by the Vancouver Aquarium since 1983. It is the only long-term natural history research commitment in Howe Sound. *(VAQ)*

located on Popham Island, the most southwesterly island in the sound. Since 1983 it has been a privately owned nature refuge overseen by the Vancouver Aquarium. The staff not only supervises the island's protection, but also monitors Howe Sound's marine life. As the only long-term natural history research commitment in the sound, it follows fish and shrimp behaviour, keeps a census of harbour seals, and monitors the behaviour of starfish and the biology of glass sponges among other projects. A major new focus is on the biology of the ling cod in the sound, especially with respect to the protected areas.

Marine parks at Porteau Cove and Whytecliff have been protected for several years through bans on removal of any sea life. An ecological reserve on Baynes Island in the Squamish River and a 987-hectare (2438-acre) preserve on Bowen Island, established in 1973, protect some land and water segments of the ecosystem. Interested groups have formed the Protect Howe Sound Society and the Howe Sound Roundtable.

The area's protectors are becoming more and more aware of its needs, but have a continuing challenge to meet.

CHAPTER 11

THE SEA TO SKY COUNTRY

Howe Sound, immediately adjoining Burrard inlet on the north is an extensive though probably useless sheet of water, the general depth being very great, while there are but few anchorages. It is almost entirely hemmed in by rugged and precipitous mountains rising abruptly from the water's edge to elevations of from 4,000 to 6,000 feet; there is no available land for the settler, and although a river of considerable size, the Squawmisht, navigable for boats, falls into its head, it leads by no useful or even practicable route into the interior of the country.

—Captain George Richards, *Vancouver Island Pilot*, 1864

Shipwrecks

Visibility was good in Vancouver harbour on October 29, 1953. The big steam tug *Dola* chugged stolidly under Lions Gate Bridge, heading for Howe Sound and Squamish and towing a barge loaded with railway cars. A wooden tug weighing 145 tonnes (160 tons) and 33 metres (109 feet) long, she was on another routine assignment. The *Dola* had been working up and down the British Columbia coast since 1907.

The weather changed after she rounded Point Atkinson and headed north. She became totally enveloped in a thick fog bank. The watch officers repeatedly sounded the whistle. The crew could hear replies from what they knew to be a large ship in the distance, but it was hidden by the fog.

Suddenly the other ship emerged from the mist and its bow sliced into the *Dola*'s side with a crash of breaking timbers. It was the Union Steamship's *Lady Cynthia*, returning to Vancouver carrying passengers from Britannia. Water rushed into the tug's hull. Second Engineer Johnson, trapped against the engine with the steamship's bow actually pressing against his chest, was barely able to pull himself free. He raced up to the deck and escaped, clambering over the *Cynthia*'s railings with the eight other crewmen.

In less than a minute, the old veteran *Dola* floated free and sank to the bottom, a hundred fathoms below. The crewmen on the barge scarcely had time to cast off the towline to prevent the tug from pulling everything down with her. The remains of the wreck still lie deep under the waves in Howe Sound, only .8 kilometres (½ mile) west of Whytecliff Park.[1]

Howe Sound's depths are the graveyard of many ships, most employed in transporting commercial cargoes. The small steamer *Nellie* was the first to sink in gale force winds in March 1891. Since that time, dozens of ocean-going vessels, mostly tugs, have burned, sunk or beached throughout the sound, many with loss of life. Some were recovered and towed to Vancouver for scrap or refitting. Many still lie where they

The tug *Emerald Straits* sank a few kilometres south of Britannia. This photo shows it being raised in 1969. *(Vancouver Maritime Museum)*

foundered, in water too deep for salvage.

One notable attempt was launched to raise the 23-metre (75-foot) tug *F.M. Yorke*. Bound for Woodfibre in April 1948 during a heavy rain and windstorm, and towing a railway barge, the ship smashed into rocks near the Defence Islands. The barge rode up onto the tug's stern, and both went under. The ferry *Bonnabelle* rescued all but one of the crew. In water about 260 metres (853 feet) deep, the wreck was abandoned. An inventive diver, John Peters, decided to attempt a unique salvage effort using a diving bell—a welded steel tube, shaped like a coffin, that was just large enough for a man to stand in. It had glass portholes and a bolted-down steel cover that was fitted with an attachment for the lifting cable. The diver had the use of a telephone and electric lights. After several narrow escapes and insurmountable difficulties during 1949, the optimistic plans were forgotten and the diving bell rusted away on land.

By the 1960s, the invention of a minisub improved the chances of salvaging wrecks. It was used during 1969 to raise the tug *Emerald Straits*, which had sunk a few kilometres south of Britannia.

Howe Sound also provides a memorial for those who love the sea. The September 4, 1978, issue of the *Coast News* had a front-page story about what was at the time the only official burial marker in British Columbia waters. Just off Gambier Island's southwest corner, a tiny island of grey granite, Steamboat Rock, was officially made the burial site for seafarers and their relatives and renamed "The Mariners' Rest." The provincial government officially sanctioned this location for the use of relatives who could scatter the ashes of their loved ones on the waters.

Point Atkinson

Every two-and-a-half hours from sundown to sunrise, Ernie Dawe or his assistant climbed the three-storey tower at Point Atkinson lighthouse to hand-wind the system of weights that revolved the flashing light. Like the lightkeepers before them, they were committed to keeping the light and foghorn operating.

Ernie Dawe had been lightkeeper since 1935, and even before his tenure a 500-candlepower oil lamp with a 5-centimetre (2-inch) mantle, similar to those used in early homesteads, had generated the light. Giant prisms, like glass Venetian blinds, encircled the lamp and increased the beam to 100,000 candlepower. During the day, Ernie had to enclose the tower's window with canvas curtains for protection from the sun's intense heat, magnified by the plate glass. One time Ernie's shirt caught on fire while he was working in the tower's top room.

The Dawe family's secluded life changed abruptly in October 1941 when the government installed a defence system at Point Atkinson, along with three others at Point Grey, Stanley Park and (First) Narrows North. Eighty men occupied newly constructed barracks in the woods behind the lighthouse and practised their gunnery skills with the Mark 1, an 8-kilogram (18 pound) cannon that stood on a concrete base in front of the radio room. A powerful searchlight mounted on a concrete bunker was ready for night reconnaissance. Manned observation posts and a radio communication system provided 24-hour-a-day surveillance. If any ship entering the harbour failed to identify itself to the patrolling naval launches, one of the land-based cannons, called "examination guns," was to fire a shot across the bows and ultimately sink the offender if it failed to stop. Fortunately, the facility never needed to defend the harbour, although a Japanese submarine allegedly shelled the Point Estevan lighthouse on Vancouver Island in June 1942.

After the war the Dawes' life returned to its peaceful routine, but they then had the benefit of the army-constructed road leading to the point. The barracks buildings, still maintained, are now used for children's camps and a nature house.

Ernie Dawe retired in 1961, the year that an electric light replaced the old oil lamp and a motor was installed to run timers controlling the lights and radio beam frequencies and the foghorn timing. The new light-keeper, Gordon Odlum, only had to climb the tower twice a day, to open and draw the curtains at dusk and dawn.

The old fog alarm, installed in 1912 and powered by internal combustion engines and air compressors with diaphones, had long been a familiar sound to many North Shore and Vancouver residents. The voice of "Old Wahoo," as some people called it, had been compared to an elephant with a cold but had become part of Vancouver's character. Electronic equipment replaced it in 1974 and the government's plan to automate its lighthouses moved a step ahead.

One insidious aspect of the light did not change, however. Because modern alloys were not available to manufacture ballbearings that could be used as its base when it was constructed, the light floated in a mercury bath. The use of mercury continued even after alloys were created and even though the danger of mercury poisoning through spills or evaporation

Donald Graham, the former lightkeeper at Point Atkinson, on the dock below the automated light, 1997. The area is now a national historic site. *(DA)*

was well documented. Donald Graham and Gerry Watson took over as lightkeepers in 1980 and each stood 12-hour watches seven days a week. Donald Graham finally refused to work with the mercury system after he had kept a three-year record of the mercury level increase in his blood and urine samples. The government replaced the mercury bath with a modern system in 1987, although some lighthouses continue to operate with the old format.

Point Atkinson's lighthouse is unique because it is so close to people, homes and the conveniences of a large city. The seemingly ideal location had its own set of problems, however, as unwanted visitors to Lighthouse Park—drunks, vandals and potential thieves—intruded on the lighthouse grounds. Picnickers also added a different dimension to the lightkeepers' job by forgetting to extinguish bonfires and dumping barbeque coals onto flammable ground. Fire watches and control were part of the lightkeepers' summer responsibilities.

In September 1994, 120 years after its construction, the lighthouse and the point of land on which it stands became a National Historic Site. Less than two years later, the federal government made good its promise to automate the system in what it called a cost-cutting move. The coast guard estimates savings from automating 18 Canadian lighthouses on the Atlantic and Pacific coasts will be $1.8 million per year. Critics of automation estimate the costs will be much higher as water safety will be jeopardized without lightkeepers on site to report people in difficulty and to aid in rescues. However, May 31, 1996, was the last day that the dedicated keepers of the Point Atkinson light supervised the safety of mariners.

Bowen Island

Hutt Island is a tree-covered, hat-shaped mound of rock about 150 metres (500 feet) off Bowen Island's northwestern corner. An uninhabited 20 hectares (49.5 acres), without a stream for drinking water, it attracts grouse and deer hunters, kayakers and canoeists to its precipitous shores.

During January 1968, the peace and quiet on nearby Bowen Island was disturbed by the sounds of piledriver installation, then shattered by the constant pounding as the machine drove pilings into Hutt Island's eastern shore. Soon afterwards, dynamite blasts rattled dishes and shook Bowen's isolated homes. Ostensibly, the piledriving company from North Vancouver was preparing the site for the first stages of a small subdivision, but a reliable source revealed that the island was initially to be levelled to about 4 metres (13 feet) above sea level and used as a rock quarry. The pilings were to support wharf construction. Bowen residents fought the project, and, over a year later, it was abandoned and the island sold.

Bowen Islanders have traditionally protected their tranquil environment strenuously against the threat of urban incursion. Their 12-kilometre-long (7.5-mile) island has attracted visitors since the late 1800s, being the closest large Howe Sound island to Vancouver, and has had the highest population of permanent residents. Concerned about the island's future development, home owners formed the Bowen Island Improvement Association in 1947, and this group has continued to monitor and influence development plans. Very supportive of the Islands Trust, it now operates under the name Bowen Island Alliance Association.

In 1958, the Black Ball Ferries installed the island's first car-loading ramp at Snug Cove. Great excitement greeted the initial load of cars landing from the ferry, the *Bainbridge*, on May 7, 1958. Until that time, steamships had freighted in all island cars, which was more expensive than the ferry cost and also meant that the cars had to stay on the island. With the arrival of ferry service, Bowen became the only Howe Sound island to be part of British Columbia's highway system, with all of its

Joan Tennant, granddaughter of Frederick A. Billington, the original pre-emptor in 1908 of the northwest corner of Bowen Island at Grafton Bay, 1996. Hutt Island can be seen in the distance. *(DA)*

attendant implications. Easier access meant more people were willing and eager to make the island their home, or at least the site of their vacation property.

One of the first residential developments was advertised as "Bowen Island Estates." In 1962 and 1963, nearly 160 lots on the former Union Steamship Company property beside Snug Cove and Deep Bay were offered for sale for $2500 each. This subdivision included 486 hectares (1200 acres) of beach, forest and meadow land, some including the former vacation cottages. It attracted buyers with its city-style services—paved roads, water, fire hydrants, electricity and telephones. A large recreational area was also planned. Most buyers made Bowen their permanent home, and some were the first of the island's commuters to Vancouver.

Other developments followed, and the 1966 inauguration of a larger car ferry, the *Bowen Queen*, carrying 60 cars plus foot passengers to and from Horseshoe Bay, encouraged more people to consider Bowen Island in their future. Property owners were having a new experience: meeting people they didn't know on the island.

More subdivision plans were submitted, including one for a development of 1000 homes with a shopping centre and another for a ski lodge with snowmaking equipment on 750-metre (2460-foot) Mount Gardner's lush green slopes. In 1969, however, the government instituted a freeze on the sale of Bowen Island Crown land, supported by the Bowen Island Improvement Association, and made plans for a land-water use study. In 1971 the Greater Vancouver Regional District (GVRD) became responsible for the island's planning. The GVRD assigned all existing privately owned land for either residential or for future development use and, in 1972, instituted a minimum 4-hectare (10-acre) lot size on unsubdivided land. In 1974 the provincial government placed Bowen under the Islands Trust's jurisdiction for land-use planning and zoning. The GVRD then became responsible for delivering local services such as recreation, water and garbage. Subdividers have received permission to develop some land, but only following the strict regulations laid down by the official bodies.

As the GVRD's principal responsibilities involved multimillion-dollar Lower Mainland sewage and water projects, holding the role of local government for Bowen did not appear to be appropriate to its mandate. In the 1980s it petitioned the provincial government to relieve it of that responsibility and offered some alternatives for consideration: Bowen Island could be annexed by West Vancouver, included in an electoral area made up of the University of British Columbia Endowment Lands and the land north of North and West Vancouver, or be part of a new regional district made up of the 13 islands under the Islands Trust's jurisdiction.

Between 1980 and 1990, the island's full-time population increased by 105 percent, to over 2200 people. Finding themselves living in one of the fastest growing areas on Howe Sound, some residents, with the support of their elected representatives, requested that the province conduct a review of options for Bowen Island's local government. As a result of this request and the GVRD's petition, the province agreed to fund such a study and in 1987 appointed a Restructure Steering Committee of Bowen Islanders who would make a recommendation to the minister of Municipal Affairs on the feasibility of a referendum. After intensive study of a number of options, the committee recommended that the question of municipal status be taken to the community voters and that an incorporation referendum be held.

Residents and property owners were divided on the issue. Some feared that the change in status would weaken the Islands Trust role and lead to the end of their rural lifestyle. Others felt that it was time to bring local government closer to the island by incorporating. In November 1991, by a margin of nearly two to one, the voters decided to stay within the control of the Islands Trust and the GVRD. Again, the GVRD approached the provincial government to look at ways in which it could be relieved of responsibility for Bowen. In 1997, the provincial government, in consultation with the elected officials on Bowen, agreed to appoint a consultant to review municipal status for the island.

Meanwhile, island residents enjoy their community. Many participate in the vibrant arts colony. They have numerous opportunities to volunteer in local groups, including organizations that record and preserve the island's history. The Davies Heritage Orchard Project will restore some of the original summer cottages, built early in the 1900s, to house summer visitors, and will revitalize the surrounding orchards.

Lions Bay

Several waterfront communities have developed north of Horseshoe Bay, attracting city people to their scenic locations and lower property prices. The largest is Lions Bay.

Probably the first resident at the site that would later become Lions Bay was the caretaker of Vancouver's St. Mark's Anglican Church Camp on Lions Beach. In the early 1920s, two small cabins, a kitchen and dormitory were the first buildings, and children arriving by boat slept in the dorm or in tents. The continuing ascents of The Lions, which had begun in 1889, were very popular with mountaineering clubs. Climbers reported that in 1923 and 1924, the caretaker permitted them to sleep overnight in "a fine camp building," where they were very comfortable and could make an early start on the mountain.

The village of Lions Bay, 11 kilometres (6 ¾ miles) north of Horseshoe Bay, had its beginning when Bob Nelson of North Vancouver visited the area by boat, discovered its unsurpassed views and undisturbed forest setting, and realized its potential. He purchased land in 1956. Foreseeing that the highway construction from Horseshoe Bay to Squamish would make his land very accessible, he subdivided his property and advertised lots for sale in January 1958. That spring the Coltart family built a summer home, and the next year Bob Nelson built his permanent home. He was joined by the Stewarts, Fairfields and Knights. The PGE Railway dropped off daily newspapers, and a single wire beside the tracks provided intermittent telephone service. As more families built homes, the essentials of community living—water supply, garbage pick-up and fire protection—had to be addressed. In 1966, the Lions Bay Water Improvement District addressed these and other needs, and in 1970, the Lions Bay Property Owners Association upgraded the very basic firefighting equipment (hoses and hydrants). The siren of the first firetruck echoed throughout the whole area and brought everyone outdoors to investigate as it travelled up and down every road. Lions Bay Volunteer Fire Department had been initiated and still competently serves the village and also Highway 99 accident scenes.

In February 1971, the community became a village with Allan M. (Curly) Stewart, one of the first residents, as mayor, with a council of aldermen.

In 1972 the residents adopted a carefully prepared community plan. In time, a small general store, post office, marina, primary school, tennis court, community hall, ambulance and, in the early 1980s, a volunteer-

Lions Bay home and garage beside Alberta Creek, after being undermined by a debris torrent in February 1983. The creek was a tiny meandering stream before the 3-metre (10-foot) wall of rocks, logs and mud washed down from the mountains. *(DA)*

operated library rounded out the village's facilities. Lions Bay Volunteer Search and Rescue team has been involved in many rescues, dozens of them searches for lost mountain climbers on the North Shore.

Also during the 1980s, a new housing development increased the population. Kelvin Grove's homes, architecturally designed to suit the contours of the mountainside, gradually dotted the land above and below the highway just south of the original Lions Bay. In 1996 the community had 1400 residents.

My husband, Bill, and I moved to Lions Bay in 1980, attracted by the country setting with fantastic views of Howe Sound only 25 minutes from downtown Vancouver. Our home in Lions Bay was a delightfully restful mecca, a daily retreat from a busy professional life in the city.

The features that made Lions Bay so attractive—its location on the side of a mountain, heavily treed land and sparkling mountain streams— also make it a perfect setting for disaster.

About 3:30 a.m. on February 11, 1983, we were startled awake by flashing lights and the roar of what sounded like dozens of freight trains rumbling past our house. We leaped out of bed, opened the drapes, and through the heavy rain could see only flashes of what appeared to be small fireballs directly out in front. Bill threw on some clothes and ran down to the road to find that our tiny Alberta Creek, three lots away and usually only an ankle-deep stream flowing through moss and ferns, had erupted into a three-metre-high (10-foot) torrent of debris—rocks, logs, stumps and mud. It roared down the mountainside, destroying the village's road culverts and the highway bridge, and blocking the railway line. All residents north of the creek were effectively marooned. The debris torrent fanned out as it neared Howe Sound, destroying three houses and burying and killing two young men who were sleeping in a trailer beside their home. We found out later that it had deposited 10,000 square metres (11,960 square yards) of material at the shoreline.

With no water or telephone (we were lucky to have electricity as the flashes had been caused by collapsing power lines), we huddled with our neighbours in our kitchen, boiling rain water for coffee and listening to the radio. We heard that most of Lions Bay had been swept into the sea (which it hadn't) and worried about not being able to contact our families.

When daylight finally revealed the devastation, dozens of people stood, numbed, staring at the pile of debris blocking our road on each side of the creek and at the rushing muddy water filling the deeply scoured-out creek bed. One man, obviously not aware of the blockage, had driven down from the higher levels, dressed in suit and tie. He stood on the edge of the mudslide, trying to call across to people on the other side to contact his office. No one could hear him above the water's roar. There was no other way that he could drive to Vancouver.

Later in the day, we heard that some homes at a higher level had telephone service and I was able to call my daughter and reassure the family that we were well, but had run out of dog biscuits for our family pet.

Concrete spillway on Harvey Creek, Lions Bay, 1997. It was built after the debris torrent in 1983 to prevent future slides from destroying homes and other property. A catchment basin above the spillway was designed to contain logs and rocks. *(DA).*

From this tragedy came community togetherness. The owners of the general store made up large batches of Chinese food for the emergency workers. Residents living south of the creek banded together to staff telephones and assist families. Neighbours who had never met before, clustered on the road in conversation. The volunteer firefighters were cheered for their efforts in reconnecting water lines and carrying out other emergency services.

This was not the first debris torrent to threaten Lions Bay and probably will not be the last. In September 1969, during a heavy rain, Harvey Creek, a few hundred metres south of Alberta Creek, nearly destroyed five houses along its banks. Only determined interventions prevented disaster.

Between 1984 and 1989, the Department of Highways built a dam and debris catchment basin on Harvey Creek, upstream from Lions Bay, at a cost of $4.4 million. It allows normal floods through, but catches the rocks, logs and mud from a debris torrent. These are then removed by a bulldozer. On Alberta Creek, a deep, vertical-walled, cement channel allows water and debris to pass through unimpeded. Its cost was $8.6 million. Two other protective structures on Charles and Magnesia Creeks cost the government $6.6 million. To date they have been effective in preventing further loss of life or damage. If that safety continues, the cost was a small price to pay.

On January 14, 1996, the residents celebrated the twenty-fifth anniversary of Lions Bay's incorporation as a municipality and raised their new Lions Bay flag to commemorate the occasion. Fittingly, it was designed by Victor Miles, a Lions Bay resident for 30 years, and is an image of the sea, snowcapped mountains and the sky.

Whistler

World-famous Whistler Mountain did not always bear that name. The early settlers at Alta Lake had nicknamed their mountain "Whistle Mountain" because of its large population of hoary marmots, small animals that emit high-pitched whistles. A 1924 map showed "London (Whistler) Mountain," but the title "London Mountain" became official in 1932. The name apparently referred to the adjacent London Mineral Claim staked in 1903 for the London & British North American Mining Company of Vancouver. Local residents, Vancouver newspapers and ski development literature continued to prefer Whistler Mountain. According to Janet Mason of the BC Geographical Names Office, that name became official in 1965 at the request of the Fitzsimmons Names Committee, partially made up of members from outdoors clubs.

The peaceful country community was also facing a major change in the 1960s. With the resort development moving ahead rapidly, workers, businesspeople and tourists urgently needed accommodation. The pace of life was accelerating and existing facilities were inadequate. Skiing introduced a challenging new era to the settlers, an era that would rapidly bring city life to the mountain village. Almost like a history film running at triple speed, the area evolved from a tiny community to a multi-million-dollar urban resort in only 30 years.

Electric power flowed for the first time when BC Hydro built the Rainbow substation in 1964. Used at first only by ski-lift developers, eventually the demand for power exceeded the supply. The growing population also needed water, and a preliminary delivery system was completed the same year.

Additional accommodation was essential and the first hotel-type buildings appeared during 1965—Highland Lodge and the Cheakamus Inn near the foot of the lift at what is now Whistler Creekside—and, on the opposite side of the highway, the first condominium, asking price $9500 per unit. At this time there were no building codes, sewer systems, police or firefighters.

The following year the new Chamber of Commerce took on the responsibilities of local government. It was hampered by the resort's inclusion in the Squamish-Lillooet Regional District. Most of the other communities in the district were small towns with totally different needs than Whistler, which was reeling under its phenomenal growth rate and related problems. In 1974 the provincial government finally recognized the need for controlled planning of this potentially huge development and instituted a land freeze, stopping all new construction. Several changes followed. Whistler became BC's first Resort Municipality. A mayor and three aldermen were elected, and one alderman was appointed by the minister of Municipal Affairs. A $6 million sewer system was begun in 1976 and a community plan was drawn up with input from the residents and businesspeople. A zoning bylaw and the Official Community Plan ensured controlled growth. Whistler again began to expand.

The government realized that the area just north of the original development held great potential. It proposed that new ski runs be developed on Blackcomb Mountain, with a town centre near the base of Whistler Mountain's north face, on the 21.5 hectares (53 acres) held in reserve as a potential Olympic village site since the bid for the 1968 Olympics. Part of the area had been a garbage dump and was later used as overflow parking for skiers using the original Whistler ski hills.

Blackcomb Mountain opened in 1980 with the help of a grant from the BC government, and the new town centre, Whistler Village, was a beehive of building activity. Hotels, boutiques, restaurants and stores were springing up to form a core of facilities for tourists. Business was booming—until a three-year recession in the 1980s paralyzed development. Plans to construct a swimming pool and ice rink that would attract summer visitors had to be shelved.

With the economic upturn in the late 1980s, development again flourished, but this time there was a concerted effort to make the resort a year-round facility and a community where parents could raise families. In the early 1990s, an ice arena, swimming pool and community

Whistler Village North, the third major stage of Whistler/Blackcomb development, 1997. The area echoes with construction noises as hotels, apartments and shops near completion. *(DA)*

centre were built at a total cost of $12.9 million, financed with money developers contributed to a development fund as part of their building agreements. The provincial government contributed $5.4 million toward the community's first comprehensive medical centre, with a major fundraising campaign in Whistler that collected money to buy additional equipment. Although the Myrtle Philip Elementary School had met the educational needs of young children for many years, a second elementary school was built in 1992. Older students had to travel 35 kilometres (22 miles) by bus to Pemberton High School until Whistler's high school was completed in 1996, with the first graduation held in June 1997.

The community enhancement plans were evidently successful, as the full-time population more than doubled between 1986 and 1991, reaching 4460 residents. Summer room rentals rose 69.5 percent to 232,455 in the 1993-1994 season. In 1995, condominiums at the base of Blackcomb Mountain cost an average of $270,000.

And the resort is still growing. Whistler Village North, a 24-hectare

(59-acre) site just north of Whistler Village, doubled the size of the village, adding shopping, residential and hotel facilities.

Most residents are enthusiastic about the lifestyle and opportunities, but for those who decided to make Whistler their home during the 1960s and 1970s, the urban life has turned them against what they had loved—a quiet, laid-back village with some of the best skiing and hiking in the world. They have gradually moved, some rather bitterly, to more remote locations, resuming the rustic life that has all but disappeared at the world class resort.

The cold wind that funnels south through the valleys, past the mountains of Garibaldi Park, absorbing icy air from the Tantalus Range glaciers, then gusts out of the opening in the mountains at the mouth of the Squamish River, has long been recognized by the Squamish people as "Mother of the Wind"—"Squamish" in the Coast Salish language. The wind's 40-knot strength, with gusts of up to 70 knots, has meant boating disasters for some and the thrill of the best windsurfing in Canada for others. The white-capped waves, glistening under the sun along the length of Howe Sound, pound into wharves and pilings along the shores, rock boats tied up in the marinas, beat against tugs struggling to keep their log booms and barges on course, and hiss along the hulls of sleek sailboats running before the wind. Sports fishers pull in their lines and head for shelter. Another glorious day around the sound.

NOTES

Throughout the text, native stories and place names related by August Jack Khahtsahlano are drawn from his interviews with Major J.S. Matthews that are detailed in Matthews' book *Conversations With Khahtsahlano, 1932-1954*. August Jack was the grandson of the Squamish Chief Khahtsahlanogh, from whom the Vancouver area of Kitsilano takes its name. All references to and translations of Squamish Native place names, and the anecdotes in chapters one and two, are from this book.

Major Matthews was the City of Vancouver's first archivist. He interviewed many early settlers in the Vancouver area, documenting their stories in his *Early Vancouver*. I drew on Matthews' interviews with or written material from Ed Baynes, J.W. Bell, Muriel Crakanthorp, Edward Goudy, W.A. Grafton, A.P. Horne, Mrs. James Walker, Elsa Wiegand, Hiram Woodward, and J.W. Woodward.

Chapter 1

1. I'd like to thank John Clague, Geological Survey of Canada, for his help with this section.

2. Dr. William H. Mathews, *Garibaldi Geology* (Vancouver: Geological Association of Canada, 1975), p. 27

3. Stephen L. Harris, *Fire and Ice: The Cascade Volcanoes*, rev. ed. (Vancouver: Douglas and McIntyre Ltd., 1980) pp. 254-256

4. D.P. Moore and W.H. Mathews, "The Rubble Creek Landslide, Southwestern British Columbia," *Canadian Journal of Earth Sciences*, vol. 15, no. 7 (July 1978), p. 1040

5. Graeme Wynne and Timothy Oke, eds., *Vancouver and Its Region* (Vancouver: UBC Press, 1992), pp. 23, 24

6. Knut R. Fladmark, *British Columbia Prehistory* (Ottawa: Archaeological Survey of Canada, National Museum of Man, 1986), pp. 13-15, 36

7. Wayne Suttles, ed., *Central Coast Salish*, vol. 7 of *Handbook of North American Indians* (Washington: Smithsonian Institution, 1990), p. 453. Information in the next five paragraphs is drawn from Suttles' book, pp. 42, 292, 462-468

8. British Columbia Provincial Archives, *Coast Salish*, vol. II of series I in the British Columbia Heritage Series (Victoria: BC Department of Education, 1966), p. 20

9. James Alexander Teit, *The Lillooet Indians*, part V of vol. II, *Jesup North Pacific Expedition*, Franz Boas, ed., of *Memoir of the American Museum of Natural History* (New York: G.E. Stechert, 1906), pp. 196-200

Chapter 2

1. E.O.S. Scholefield and F.W. Howay, *British Columbia from the Earliest Times to the Present*, vol. 1 (Vancouver: Clarke Publishing Co., 1914), pp. 12-13

2. E. von Richthofen, "The Spanish Toponyms of the British Columbia Coast" in *Onomastica* #26 (1963), p. 14

3. George Vancouver, *A Voyage of Discovery 1791-1795*, vol. III (London: Robinson and Edwards, 1798), pp. 583-586. All quotes from Vancouver are taken from this book.

4. Archibald Menzies, *Menzies' Journal of Vancouver's Voyage April to October, 1792*, edited with botanical and ethnological notes by C.F. Newcombe (Victoria: Archives of British Columbia, 1923), p. 61

5. Peter Puget, *A Log of the proceedings of HMS Discovery, January 4, 1791 to January 14, 1793*, Public Records Office (London), Group: Admiralty, p. 109

6. Scholefield, *British Columbia*, p. 113

7. G.V.P. Akrigg and Helen Akrigg, *British Columbia Chronicle, 1778-1846* (Vancouver: Discovery Press, 1975), p. 108

8. Richard Charles Mayne, *Four Years in British Columbia and Vancouver Island* (London: John Murray, 1862), p. 10

Chapter 3

1. G.V.P. Akrigg and Helen Akrigg, *British Columbia Chronicle, 1847-1871* (Vancouver: Discovery Press, 1977), pp. 104, 105, 137

2. Great Britain, Parliament, *Papers Relative to the Affairs of British Columbia*, part I, 1859, p. 17

3. Dr. John Sebastian Helmcken, *Reminiscences of Dr. J.S. Helmcken*, ed. Dorothy Blakey Smith (Vancouver: University of British Columbia, 1975), pp. 82, 83

4. Akrigg, *Chronicle, 1847-1871*, p. 166

5. Details of McKay's expedition can be found in Great Britain, Parliament, *Papers Relative to the Affairs of British Columbia*, parts I & II, 1859.

6. Akrigg, *Chronicle, 1847-1871*, p. 168

7. British Columbia Archives and Records, Colonial Correspondence, Howe Sound Copper Mines Ltd., March 2, 1870

8. British Columbia, "Report of Minister of Mines for the Year 1874," *Sessional Papers, 1875*, p. 578

Chapter 4

1. G.V.P. Akrigg and Helen Akrigg, *British Columbia Chronicle, 1847-1871* (Vancouver: Discovery Press, 1977), p. 101

2. Richards' report of his survey was published by the British Admiralty in *Vancouver Island Pilot* (London: Hydrographic Office, 1864).

3. Captain John R. Walbran, *British Columbia Coast Names, 1592-1906* (Vancouver: The Library's Press, 1971), p. 205

4. Alan Morley, *Vancouver: From Milltown to Metropolis* (Vancouver: Mitchell Press, 1961), p. 21

5. Ibid., pp. 25, 26

6. Information on land leases, pre-emptions, and the voters' list can be found in the British Columbia, *Sessional Papers* for the year in question.

7. Lester R. Peterson, *The Gibson's Landing Story* (Peter Martin Books, 1962), p. 26

8. Ibid., p. 23

9. Details on the construction of the Pemberton Trail come from the British Columbia *Sessional Papers* from 1873/74, 1877, and 1878.

10 Lorraine Harris, *Halfway to the Goldfields* (North Vancouver: J.J. Douglas Ltd., 1977), p. 23, and the Vancouver *Province*, May 23, 1936

11. Frances Decker, Margaret Fougberg and Mary Ronayne, *Pemberton: The History of a Settlement* (Pemberton: Pemberton Pioneer Women, 1977), p. 73

Chapter 5

1. Major J.S. Matthews, *Early Vancouver*, vol. 3 (Victoria: Provincial Archives of British Columbia, 1932), p. 365

2. The early history of Point Atkinson lighthouse was recounted by Donald Graham in *Keepers of the Light* (Madeira Park: Harbour Publishing Company, 1985), pp. 64-67

3. Major J.S. Matthews' records, Add mss 54, file 05029, J.W. Woodward correspondence to J.S. Matthews, January 12, 1940, Vancouver Archives

4. G.V.P. Akrigg and Helen Akrigg, *British Columbia Chronicle, 1847-1871* (Vancouver: Discovery Press, 1977), p. 404

5. Bruce Ramsey, *Britannia: The Story of a Mine* (Britannia Beach: Britannia Beach Community Club, 1967), pp. 18, 19

6. Francis J. Van Den Wyngaert, *The West Howe Sound Story, 1886-1976* (Vancouver: privately published, 1976), p. 5

7. Major J.S. Matthews' records, Add mss 54, vol. 1-13, file 01802, conversation with W.A. Grafton, May 4, 1939, Vancouver Archives

8. Ken Drushka, *Working in the Woods* (Madeira Park: Harbour Publishing, 1992), p. 44

9. Major J.S. Matthews' records, Add mss 54, conversation with W.A. Grafton, September 18, 1938, Vancouver Archives

10. Major J.S. Matthews' records, Add mss 54, file 03067, conversation with A.P. Horne, Vancouver Archives

11. Irene Howard, *Bowen Island, 1872-1972* (Bowen Island: Bowen Island Historians, 1973), p. 33

12. George B. Baynes and Edgar G. Baynes, *Pioneer of the West, 1870-1956* (Vancouver: privately published pamphlet, 1957), p. 2

13. J.M. Cummings and J.W. McCammon, *Clay and Shale Deposits of British Columbia*, Bulletin #30, British Columbia Department of Mines and Petroleum Resources, 1952

Chapter 6

1. Gerald A. Rushton, *Whistle Up the Inlet* (Vancouver: Douglas and McIntyre, 1974), pp. 17, 18

2. Public Works reports can be found in the British Columbia, *Sessional Papers* or *Public Accounts* for the year in question.

3. Frances Decker, Margaret Fougberg and Mary Ronayne, *Pemberton: The History of a Settlement* (Pemberton: Pemberton Pioneer Women, 1977), p. 76

4. Frank Burnett, *Westward Ho!* magazine (December 1908), p. 428

5. Irene Howard, *Bowen Island 1872-1972* (Bowen Island: Bowen Island Historians, 1973), p. 43

6. *Ibid.*, p. 47

7. George H. Melvin, *Post Offices of British Columbia, 1858-1970* (Vernon: Wayside Press Ltd., 1972)

8. Howard, *Bowen Island*, p. 166

Chapter 7

1. Ken Drushka, *Working in the Woods* (Madeira Park: Harbour Publishing, 1992), p. 94

2. Gerald A. Rushton, *Whistle Up the Inlet* (Vancouver: Douglas and McIntyre, 1974), pp. 87, 88

3. Anne McMahon, *The Whistler Story* (West Vancouver: A. McMahon Pub., 1980), pp. 33, 34

4. Bruce Ramsey, *PGE: Railway to the North* (Vancouver: Mitchell Press, 1962)

5. Adolf Hungry Wolf, *Route to the Cariboo: PGE/BC Rail* (Skookumchuck: Canadian Caboose Press, 1994)

6. Ellen Frith and Peter Trower, *Rough and Ready Times: The History of Port Mellon* (Gibsons: Glassford Press, 1993)

Chapter 8

1. Ken Drushka, *Against Wind and Weather* (Vancouver: Douglas and McIntyre, 1981), p. 90

2. Ruth Kozak, *The Admiral's Island*, c. 1962, British Columbia Archives, p. 4

3. G.H. Pousett, *The Keats Island Story* (Vancouver: Keats Camps, 1986)

4. Anne McMahon, *The Whistler Story* (West Vancouver: McMahon Pub., 1980), p. 18

5. Gerald A. Rushton, *Whistle Up the Inlet* (Vancouver: Douglas and McIntyre, 1974), p. 102

6. McMahon, *Whistler Story*, p. 25

Chapter 10

1. "Cheakamus-Clowhom," BC Hydro pamphlet, BC Hydro Library, H0270

2. The *Summary of Proceedings* of Howe Sound Watershed Environmental Science Workshops and Public Meetings (Ottawa: Environment Canada, 1992). This report was used as a reference throughout this section.

3. Dennis Deans, "Squamish Estuary Management Process," a paper read at the Howe Sound Watershed Environmental Science Workshops and Public Meetings, *Summary of Proceedings* (Ottawa: Environment Canada, 1992), p. 14

Chapter 11

1. Fred Rogers, *Shipwrecks of British Columbia* (Vancouver: Douglas and McIntyre, 1973), p. 239

SELECTED
BIBLIOGRAPHY

Akrigg, G.V.P., and Helen Akrigg. *British Columbia Chronicle, 1778-1846*. Vancouver: Discovery Press, 1975.

—————. *British Columbia Chronicle, 1847-1871*. Vancouver: Discovery Press, 1977.

Anderson, Alexander Caulfield. *History of the Northwest Coast*. British Columbia Archives.

Armstrong, John. *Vancouver Geology*. Vancouver: Geological Association of Canada, 1990.

Backus, Harriet Fish. *Tomboy Bride*. Boulder: Pruett Publishing Company, 1969.

Baynes, George B., and Edgar G. Baynes. *Pioneer of the West, 1870-1956*. Vancouver: privately published pamphlet, 1957.

BC Mountaineer. March 1923.

Bowen Island Archives, Correspondence and photographs.

British Columbia. *Sessional Papers, 1873-1902*.

British Columbia Archives and Record Service. Colonial Correspondence. Howe Sound Copper Mines Ltd. March 2, 1870.

—————. Correspondence Outward.

—————. *Coast Salish*. British Columbia Heritage Series, series I, vol. II. Victoria: BC Department of Education, 1966.

British Columbia, Ministry of Forests. *Timber Licenses, March 1884 to May 1899*.

Burnett, Frank. *Westward Ho!* magazine (Vancouver). December 1908.

Burton, Pierre. *The Great Railway*. Toronto: McClelland and Stewart Ltd., 1972.

Canada. Department of Agriculture. "Province of British Columbia: Information for Intending Settlers." 1886.

Cheakamus–Clowhom. BC Hydro pamphlet. BC Hydro Library Information.

Cummings, J.M., and J.W. McCammon. *Clay and Shale Deposits of British Columbia*. British Columbia Department of Mines and Petroleum Resources. Bulletin #30. 1952.

Davis, Charles H. *The Vancouver Book.* Vancouver: J.J. Douglas Ltd., 1976.

Decker, Frances, Margaret Fougberg, and Mary Ronayne. *Pemberton: The History of a Settlement.* Pemberton: Pemberton Pioneer Women, 1977.

"Diamond Head Chalet: Demolition by Neglect?" In *Heritage BC Newsletter*, Fall 1992.

Downie, Major William. *Hunting for Gold: Reminiscences of Personal Experience.* San Francisco: The California Publishing Company, 1893.

Drushka, Ken. *Against Wind and Weather.* Vancouver: Douglas and McIntyre, 1981.

——————. *Working in the Woods.* Madeira Park: Harbour Publishing Company, 1992.

Dunal, Patrick A. *The School Record: A Guide to Government Archives Relating to Public Education in British Columbia, 1842-1946.* Victoria: BC Ministry of Government Services (BCARS), 1992.

Elphinstone Pioneer Museum, Gibsons, BC. Correspondence and photographs.

Ferguson, Alan, and Michael McPhee. *Howe Sound Watershed Environmental Science Workshop and Public Meetings, October-November, 1991, Summary of Proceedings.* Ottawa: Environment Canada (Pacific and Yukon Region), December 1991.

Fisher, Robin, and Hugh Johnston, eds. *From Maps to Metaphors: The Pacific World of George Vancouver.* Vancouver: UBC Press, 1993.

Frith, Ellen, and Peter Trower. *Rough and Ready Times: The History of Port Mellon.* Gibsons: Glassford Press, 1993.

Graham, Donald. *Keepers of the Light.* Madeira Park: Harbour Publishing Company, 1985.

Great Britain, Parliament. *Papers Relative to the Affairs of British Columbia, Parts I and II.* 1859.

Harnett, Legh, Esq. *Two Lectures on British Columbia.* Victoria: Higgins and Long, 1868.

Harris, Lorraine. *Halfway to the Goldfields.* North Vancouver: J.J. Douglas Ltd., 1977.

Harris, Stephen L. *Fire & Ice: The Cascade Volcanoes*, rev. ed. Vancouver: Douglas and McIntyre, 1980.

Helmcken, Dr. J.S. *Reminiscences of Dr. John Sebastian Helmcken.* Ed. Dorothy Blakey Smith. Vancouver: University of British Columbia, 1975.

Horticultural Society and Fruit Growers' Association of British Columbia. *Annual Reports, 1891-1893.*

Howard, Irene. *Bowen Island 1872-1972*. Bowen Island: Bowen Island Historians, 1973.

Hydrographic Office, Admiralty. *Vancouver Island Pilot*. London: Hydrographic Office, 1864.

Keeling, T.J. Collection. City of Vancouver Archives.

Kimmett, Bill. "Escape to Passage." *The Cottage Magazine* (Victoria). Nov./Dec. 1995.

Kozak, Ruth. *The Admiral's Island*. BC Archives.

Lord, John K. *The Naturalist in Vancouver Island and British Columbia*. London, 1886.

Matthews, Major J.S. *Early Vancouver*. Vols 1-3. Victoria: BC Archives, 1932.

——————. Add mss 54, Vancouver City Archives.

——————. *Conversations with Khahtsahlano 1932-1935*. Vancouver: City of Vancouver Archives, 1955.

Mayne, Richard Charles. *Four Years in British Columbia and Vancouver Island*. London: John Murray, 1862.

McMahon, Anne. *The Whistler Story*. West Vancouver: McMahon Pub., 1980.

Melvin, George H. *The Post Offices of British Columbia, 1858-1970*. Vernon: Wayside Press Ltd., 1972.

Menzies, Archibald. *Menzies' Journal of Vancouver's Voyage April to October, 1792*. Edited with botanical and ethnological notes by C.F. Newcombe. Victoria: BC Archives, 1923.

Menzies, C.P.O. "Northwest Coast Middens." In *The Great Fraser Midden*. Vancouver: Vancouver Art, Historical and Scientific Association, 1948.

Moore, D.P., and W.H. Mathews. "The Rubble Creek Landslide, Southwestern British Columbia." In *Canadian Journal of Earth Sciences*, vol.15, no.7. July 1978.

Morley, Alan. *Vancouver: From Milltown to Metropolis*. Vancouver: Mitchell Press, 1961.

Peterson, Lester R. *The Gibson's Landing Story*. Peter Martin Books Canada, 1962.

Pousett, G.H. *The Keats Island Story*. Vancouver: Keats Camps, 1986.

Puget, Peter. *A Log of the proceedings of HMS Discovery, January 1791 to January 14, 1793*. Public Records Office (London).

Ramsey, Bruce. *Britannia: The Story of a Mine*. Britannia Beach: Britannia Beach Community Club, 1967.

——————. *PGE: Railway to the North*. Vancouver: Mitchell Press, 1962.

Roedde, Gus. "A View of Horseshoe Bay." In *Vancouver Historical Society Newsletter*, vol. 16, no. 2. October 1976.

Rogers, Fred. *Shipwrecks of British Columbia*. Vancouver: Douglas and McIntyre, 1973.

Rushton, Gerald A. *Whistle Up the Inlet*. Vancouver: Douglas and McIntyre, 1974.

Scholefield, E.O.S., and F.W. Howay, *British Columbia from the Earliest Times to the Present*. Vol I. Vancouver: Clarke Publishing Company, 1914.

Smith, F.H., *Cabins, Camps, and Climbs: The Mountaineer, 50th Anniversary 1907-1957*. Chapman and Warwick Ltd., 1958.

Suttles, Wayne. *Central Coast Salish*. Vol. 7 of *Handbook of North American Indians*. Washington: Smithsonian Institution, 1990.

Sweet, Arthur F. *Islands in Trust*. Lantzville: Oolichan Books, 1988.

Teit, James Alexander. *The Lillooet Indians*. Part V of Vol. II of *Memoir of the American Museum of Natural History*. New York: G.E. Stechert, 1906.

Thurber Consultants Ltd. *Debris Torrent and Flooding Hazards, Highway 99, Howe Sound*. Report to Ministry of Transportation and Highways, British Columbia, April 1983.

Vancouver, George. *A Voyage of Discovery, 1791-1795*. Vol.III. London: Robinson and Edwards, 1798.

Van Den Wyngaert, Francis J. *The West Howe Sound Story, 1886-1976*. Vancouver: privately published, 1976.

von Richtofen, E. "The Spanish Toponyms of the British Columbia Coast." In *Onomastica* #26 (Winnipeg). 1963.

Walbran, Captain John T. *British Columbia Coast Names, 1592-1906*. Vancouver: The Library's Press, 1971.

White, Mary S. *A History of the Sannie Transportation Company Ltd., 1922-1954*. Vancouver Archives, 1957.

Wynne, Graeme, and Timothy Oke, eds. *Vancouver and Its Region*. Vancouver: UBC Press, 1992.

INDEX